THE IMPLICIT NORMS OF RABBINIC JUDAISM

The Bedrock of a Classical Religion

Jacob Neusner

Studies in Judaism

University Press of America,® Inc.
Lanham · Boulder · New York · Toronto · Oxford

Copyright © 2006 by
University Press of America,® Inc.
4501 Forbes Boulevard
Suite 200
Lanham, Maryland 20706
UPA Acquisitions Department (301) 459-3366

PO Box 317
Oxford
OX2 9RU, UK

All rights reserved
Printed in the United States of America
British Library Cataloging in Publication Information Available

Library of Congress Control Number: 2005935824
ISBN 978-0-7618-3383-3

∞™ The paper used in this publication meets the minimum
requirements of American National Standard for Information
Sciences—Permanence of Paper for Printed Library Materials,
ANSI Z39.48—1984

Studies in Judaism

EDITOR

Jacob Neusner
Bard College

EDITORIAL BOARD

Alan J. Avery-Peck
College of the Holy Cross

Herbert Basser
Queens University

Bruce D. Chilton
Bard College

José Faur
Bar Ilan University

William Scott Green
University of Rochester

Mayer Gruber
Ben-Gurion University of the Negev

Günter Stemberger
University of Vienna

James F. Strange
University of South Florida

TABLE OF CONTENTS

PREFACE vii

1. DEFINING THE HUMAN CONDITION: ABOT 1

    i. The Document and its Program: Recurrent Questions 1
    ii. To whom, and for whom, does the document speak? Propositions and preoccupations 7
    iii. Implicit truths 8

2. THE CATEGORICAL STRUCTURE OF KNOWLEDGE: THE MISHNAH 11

    i. The Document and its Program: Recurrent Questions 11
    ii. To whom, and for whom, does the document speak? Propositions and preoccupations 17
    iii. Implicit truths 22

3. THE LAWS OF INTELLECT: SIFRA 25

    i. The Document and its Program: Recurrent Questions 25
    ii. To whom, and for whom, does the document speak? Propositions and preoccupations 32
    iii. Implicit truths 33

4. THE LAWS OF HISTORY: GENESIS RABBAH 35

    i. The Document and its Program: Recurrent Questions 35
    ii. To whom, and for whom, does the document speak? Propositions and preoccupations 48
    iii. Implicit truths 49

5. THE LAWS OF SOCIETY: LEVITICUS RABBAH 51

    i. The Document and its Program: Recurrent Questions 51
    ii. To whom, and for whom, does the document speak? Propositions and preoccupations 63
    iii. Implicit truths 64

6. THE CELESTIAL LAWS: PESIQTA DERAB KAHANA 67

    i. The Document and its Program: Recurrent Questions 67

	ii.	To whom, and for whom, does the document speak? Propositions and preoccupations 76
	iii.	Implicit truths 78
7.	Knowing God: Lamentations Rabbah 81	
	i.	The Document and its Program: Recurrent Questions 81
	ii.	To whom, and for whom, does the document speak? Propositions and preoccupations 88
	iii.	Implicit truths 88
8.	Loving, and Being Loved by, God: Song of Songs Rabbah 95	
	i.	The Document and its Program: Recurrent Questions 95
	ii.	To whom, and for whom, does the document speak? Propositions and preoccupations 98
	iii.	Implicit truths 100
9.	The Norms of Conviction of Rabbinic Judaism: Orthodoxy and Heresy 109	
	i.	Principal Elements of Orthodox Doctrine 109
	ii.	The Orthodox Definition of Heresy 111
	iii.	Borderlines 112

Preface

Implicit norms of law and theology governed in Rabbinic Judaism from the onset of its canon in the Mishnah (concluded at ca. 200) to its climax in the Talmud of Babylonia four centuries later. And those norms of conviction and conception prevailed start to finish in a complete system logically present, if not fully realized, from the very beginning of the canon with the Mishnah. Accordingly, norms of belief, not only behavior, governed in the canonical documents of Rabbinic Judaism and defined orthodox and heterodoxy for that Judaism.

That fact, set forth in these pages for eight principal documents, contradicts the prevailing position on the matter. That doctrinal orthodoxy characterized Rabbinic Judaism as a system from the very outset of its canonical writings and prevailed to the end of the formative age precipitates debate. While in describing Rabbinic Judaism people generally attribute to the texts of proper conduct the status of norms of behavior expected of all Israelites, debate persists on whether there were, in addition, norms of belief that demanded assent. Can we identify orthodox doctrine that by its presence defined heresy as well? Professors Marc Kellner, Daniel Boyarin, Menachem Fisch, and Marc B. Shapiro, have responded with a negative answer.[1] Boyarin and Fisch for late antiquity, Kellner and Shapiro for medieval theology, maintain that Rabbinic Judaism adopted a latitudinarian policy toward matters of belief, tolerating, as valid, all Israelites, even though sinful. The Rabbinic texts attest to conflict, with disagreements recorded concerning matters great and small; orthodoxy and rarely, it is alleged, does heresy come to definition.[2] For Rabbinic Judaism as a system of thought that characterization is counter-intuitive, since a broad range of norms self-evidently governed conduct and matters of conviction alike, e.g., God is one, pork is forbidden, to take self-evident norms of belief and behavior. But if it is alleged in these pages that norms of conviction, not only conduct, govern, how are we to identify them?

Here I answer that question by asking, what are the theological premises upon which documents of the Rabbinic canon builds its construction and do these premises cohere in a tight theological system? I answer by identifying the principles that had to govern for a given composition to be articulated, for a particular composite to be assembled. Those premises at the foundations of the canonical documents prove not episodic but coherent. Their cogency forms the evidence of what is normative in attitude, not only in action: the givens upon which all allegations rest, the matters of consensus and presumed uniformity.

The documents speak — so it is universally maintained — for the community of the Rabbinic sages that sponsored them, not for individuals alone or mainly, and schismatic opinion is signaled in one way or another. Hence we stand on firm ground in claiming that the premises and presuppositions of a document represent the consensus of the Rabbinic sages: the implicit norms of attitude and action. Canonical orthodoxy and heresy come to definition in those norms. How individuals conformed, and what institutions functioned to enforce conformity, do not figure in this account. It suffices to show that orthodoxy and heresy constituted native categories of the Rabbinic system of thought inherent in principal documents of the canon.

The answers — the components of the Rabbinic program of orthodox belief and hence also heresy that the documents yield — are not generic but particular to the respective documents and their programs, respectively. Working in each case from the surface to the foundations, I show that the documents of Rabbinic Judaism bear implicit testimony to givens, premises and propositions that demanded affirmation before the articulated program of a given compilation can have been contemplated, before the sentences of those documents can have been written. I examine eight principal documents of formative Judaism to identify the norms of theological conviction that are implicit in those writings, viewed one by one, then (in Chapter Nine) all together. In that way I answer the question, what did someone have to believe *or know as fact* in order rationally to write or to read this writing? The answer to that question defines orthodoxy and, willy-nilly, heresy.

The documents prove diverse in character, severally taking up distinctive questions, jointly intersecting only in general. The chapter titles signal the singular propositions I maintain are implicit. But the premises inherent in each cohere in a cogent system. Not only so, but what concerns me are not generic propositions, e.g., God is one, just and merciful — but particular ones: there is a judge and judgment. Each document accordingly defines its own program and therefore also attests to its distinctive premises, yielding the questions to which right doctrines — orthodox norms — are addressed.

What of the context of orthodoxy and heresy in the ambient politics and culture? This study does not pursue historical questions of the Israelite social order, e.g., when did a given document come to closure and how did the framers of that document respond to issues of their own times? Since at issue is the theological definition of norms of conviction alongside established norms of conduct, we are not concerned with the order or the dates of the documents that are interrogated as to their data. The range of premises, the givens as to the human situation, God's encounter with Israel and Israel's encounter with God, for example, responds to the inner logic of the Rabbinic system — a vast recapitulation in a systematic and philosophical and exegetical mode of thought of Scripture's episodic laws and narratives. The Rabbinic sages took over and made their own Scripture's revealed facts, processing them into regularities of law and theology alike.[3] The human situation, the organization of knowledge, the interplay of reason and revelation and so on — these responses to canonical documents, Abot, the Mishnah, Sifra respond to timeless logic, not to exigencies of place or circumstance. That is why the date of closure of a given document and the sequence in which documents took shape play no role in this account of the premises of Rabbinic Judaism: I mean, the dogmas that all together defined the norms of belief alongside the articulated norms of behavior.

Nonetheless, the canon of Rabbinic Judaism in its formative age, commencing with the Mishnah at ca. 200 and concluding with the Bavli at ca. 600, did take shape in a determinate age and circumstance. While we deal with logic beyond the limits of time and space, we do gain perspective on the result when we situate the canon in its time. For while contemplating a timeless realm of revealed rules of conduct and conviction, the Rabbinic sages willy-nilly responded to a particular circumstance of politics and consequent religious consciousness. Circumstances contributed to the definition of self-evidence of the premises that, document by document, the interior logic dictated.

In the first six centuries of the Common Era the dominant Judaism turned from a tangible, sturdy state-cult centered on Temple sacrifices into a fragile religion realized in voluntary communities of consensual intellect. What had been sustained by the corporate community and its poll-taxes now would be nourished through prayer and study. What had been public and institutional gave way to what was private and intangible. The communal and obligatory shifted to what was personal and votive. The Judaism that emerged in the centuries between the destruction of the Temple in 70 and the advent of Islam in 640 proved normative and remains paramount even today.

Unfortunately, we cannot reconstruct the step-by—step history of that transition from a state and public to a private and ultimately personal religion and from worship through public sacrifice to individual acts of piety. The continuous, linear history of Judaism at the turn of the centuries before and after 1 C.E. eludes description. No single Judaism left an unfolding corpus of sources from before 70 to the advent of Islam. Rather, we have two large blocks of writings, unconnected with one another, and a body of archaeological and liturgical data of uncertain venue and consequence. The period down to ca. 70 C.E. is represented by episodic chapters produced by discrete groups out of communion with one another, and the groups recorded by those writings did not survive 70. Then commences a coherent, unfolding literary tradition set forth by a single group from 70 C.E. to 640, and those documents, reaching closure successively from the end of the second century to the seventh, connect with Scripture but not with records that reached closure before 70.

Describing Judaism in, say, 66 C.E., on the eve of the cataclysm of the destruction of the Second Temple in 70, and in the millennium that followed accordingly yields discontinuous and incongruent pictures. All encompass various communities calling themselves Israel, in the setting of sizable, diverse Jewish populations spread through the ancient world in the Roman and Parthian empires. An incoherent body of writings for the period before 70 portrays multiple Judaisms, intersecting and overlapping but always competing. The picture of a continuous, unitary structure that emerges six centuries later presents striking contrasts. The extant sources both before and after the seventh century portray a single group represented by a determinate canon of writings. These all together set forth a cogent and complete religious system, in which each extant piece of evidence finds a comfortable place. The state of the evidence accounts for the difference between the picture of diversity of 70 and the account of uniformity of 640.

Not only does the history of the competing Judaic religious communities of the formative age elude us, but also we cannot characterize the state of Israelite opinion, the social world of the entire population of Jews viewed as a single religious community. We have little evidence of popular opinion, and what we do have yields obscurity. External observers portray the Judaism they anticipate on the strength of Scripture and little more than that. We cannot speak of the condition of Judaism as the construction of a single community of faith. Accordingly, the social condition of Judaism, viewed as a collection of intersecting and competing religious communities sharing some common traits and differing on many is inaccessible.

But that does not mean we cannot trace the formation of any embodiment of Judaic religious consciousness in the period from 70 to 640. What we can and in these pages do undertake is to trace, as documents portray them, some of the critical testimonies to the consciousness of Rabbinic Judaism in its formative age. We can describe what was at stake in documents, the human situation implicit in them, the logic that animates them. We answer the question, what at the foundations was at stake in this piece of writing? This we do by characterizing the primary concerns, the generative tensions and recurrent preoccupations, of documents of the Rabbinic canon. Taking the canonical documents one by one and describing each as systematic and cogent, we are able to interrogate its composers and compositors as to their premises: what did they know as fact, demand as faith? These are the authors of the individual compositions that comprise the whole, the compilers or redactors who chose and arranged and imposed their judgments upon whatever they received and transformed the whole into a coherent statement. We ask questions that elicit pictures of critical tensions, recurrent concerns, attested by a given document's compilers. Viewing the document they produced as evidence of the world that they conceived and imagined, we are able to characterize how they imagined the age in which they flourished. For in their imagination they reconstructed that age and its consequential events in dialogue with the received tradition of the continuous community of masters and disciples. That process affords entry into the imagination of the sages represented by a particular piece of writing.

How, exactly, do I propose systematically to characterize the Rabbinic documents, to identify their critical tensions and generative questions, severally and jointly? The answer is, by identifying the question or questions that a given document answers. To whom, and for whom, does it speak? And what are the premises that govern the responses to those questions? The documentary traits that pertain prove substantive are these: what propositions recur, in various formulations to be sure, and what preoccupations predominate, in a given document? To answer these questions, compilation by compilation, the program of the document takes priority, its formal and logical traits are subordinated, and the preoccupations and points of tension afford answers to the question, what is at stake in this statement? That is where I find the theological and philosophical contents of orthodoxy: right doctrine, everywhere definitive, as attested by the canon of Rabbinic Judaism.

Readers will reasonably wonder, what of the Bavli? It forms the principal source for stories adduced in evidence by those who argue that Rabbinic Judaism adopted a latitudinarian position on matters of right doctrine, e.g., Fisch and Boyarin most recently. But they do not characterize the document as a whole, they merely cite passages that are episodic and singular — and ambiguous in their implications. So the question arises: Can we identify the Bavli's implicit norms, classify them, and show how they impose an orthodoxy of thought upon the exposition of the law? I follow my instincts in thinking that modes of normative *analysis* governed, signaled by norms of rhetoric that prevail throughout, and these rules of rational analysis transcend, are not limited to, the rules of dialectical argument commonly adduced[4] in evidence of the way in which the Bavli governed right thinking. Further work beckons: *normative analysis in the Bavli, a systematic catalogue.*

I enjoyed conversing on the problem of this monograph with my colleagues, Professors Bruce D. Chilton, Bard College, and William Scott Green, University of Rochester.

Jacob Neusner
Bard College
Annandale-on-Hudson, New York 12504
neusner@webjogger.net

ENDNOTES

[1] See Menachem Kellner, *Must a Jew Believe Anything?* Portland, OR., 1999: Littman Library of Jewish Civilization. Daniel Boyarin, *Border Lines. The Partition of Judaeo-Christianity,* Philadelphia, 2004: University of Pennsylvania Press. Menachem Fisch, *Rational Rabbis. Science and Talmudic Culture.* Bloomington, IN, 1997: Indiana University Press. And see for medieval norms Marc B. Shapiro, *The Limits of Orthodox Theology. Maimonides' Thirteen Principles Reappraised.* Portland, OR., 2004: Littman Library of Jewish Civilization

[2] *Contours of Coherence in Rabbinic Judaism.* Leiden, 2005: E. J. Brill. I-II.

[3] That is demonstrated in my *The Theology of the Oral Torah. Revealing the Justice of God.* Kingston and Montreal, 1999: McGill-Queen's University Press and Ithaca, 1999: Cornell University Press and *The Theology of the Halakhah.* Leiden, 2001: E. J. Brill. Brill Reference Library of Ancient Judaism.

[4] See for example my *Jerusalem and Athens: The Congruity of Talmudic and Classical Philosophy.* Leiden, 1997: E. J. Brill. *Supplements to the Journal for the Study of Judaism.*

1

Defining the Human Condition: Abot

I. THE DOCUMENT AND ITS PROGRAM: RECURRENT QUESTIONS

Tractate Abot, conventionally dated at ca. 250 C.E.,[1] on the surface appears to be a miscellaneous collection of sayings. But a second glance yields a different result. The document proves to form a theological system fully exposed. The sayings cohere and recapitulate the very category-formations that would define Rabbinic Judaism in the first six centuries of the Common Era.[2]

A claim for system and logic must set forth what is at the center of matters and holds the whole together.[3] This collection of episodic aphorisms forms a melancholy meditation on the human condition of the individual Israelite. Corporate Israel and its historical fate never frame the issue. The problem facing the framer of the document — provoked by the logic of monotheism — is succinctly stated: "We do not have in hand an explanation either for the prosperity of the wicked or for the suffering of the righteous" (4:15). The resolution of the paradox of palpable injustice — the prosperity of the wicked more than the suffering of the righteous — is in the doctrine of life beyond the grave. Individual existence does not end in death. There is a world to come, which affords eternal life to the righteous but which excludes those who are wicked in this world.

In tractate Abot that eternal life is afforded in a juridical procedure, a trial, to individuals in response to their conduct in this life. "This world is like an antechamber before the world to come. Get ready in the antechamber, so you can go into the great hall." How to prepare? "Better is a single moment spent in penitence and good deeds in this world than the whole of the world to come. And better is a single moment of inner peace in the world to come than the whole of a lifetime spent in this world" (4:16-17). The world to come then forms the reward for those that live humbly and righteously.

Above all, Heaven knows what mortals do and keeps a record for each one, with consequences that follow from right conduct, and punishment for wrong. Thus "Be meticulous in a small religious duty as in a large one, for you do not know what sort of reward is coming for any of the various religious duties. And reckon with the loss required in carrying out a religious duty against the reward for doing it, and the reward for committing a transgression against the loss for doing it. And keep your eye on three things, so you will not come into the clutches of transgression: Know what is above you: An eye which sees, and an ear which hears, and all your actions are written down in a book" (2:1). "And know before whom you work, for your employer can be depended upon to pay your wages for what you can do" (2:14). God is an active presence everywhere, and prayer is addressed to a listening ear: "when you pray, don't treat your praying as a matter of routine. But let it be a plea for mercy and supplication before the Omnipresent, blessed be he" (2:13). The Israelite lives in an enchanted world, where everything he says and does counts.

Accordingly, a coherent, compelling picture of the human situation emerges. "Those who are born are destined to die, and those who die are destined for resurrection. And the living are destined to be judged — so as to know, to make known, and to confirm that he is God, he is the one who forms, he is the one who creates, he is the one who understands, he is the one who judges, he is the one who gives evidence, he is the one who brings suit, and he is the one who is going to make the ultimate judgment. Blessed be he, for before him are not guile, forgetfulness, respect for persons, bribe taking, for everything is his. And know that everything is subject to reckoning. And do not let your evil impulse persuade you that Sheol is a place of refuge for you. For despite your wishes were you formed, despite your wishes were you born, despite your wishes do you live, despite your wishes do you die, and despite your wishes are you going to give a full accounting before the King of kings of kings, the Holy One, blessed be he" (4:22). The key to the document's message thus is that there is justice and there is a judge, and all who live are subject to retribution for their deeds: "He saw a skull floating on the water and said to it, 'Because you drowned others, they drowned you, and in the end those who drowned you will be drowned.'"

Where is the justice in all this? A simple doctrine accounts for the responsibility of each individual for every action. Man is accountable for what he does because he has free choice: "Everything is foreseen, and free choice is given. In goodness the world is judged. And all is in accord with the abundance of deeds. All is handed over as a pledge, And a net is cast over all the living. The store is open, the storekeeper gives credit, the account book is open, and the hand is writing. Whoever wants to borrow may come and borrow. The charity collectors go around every day and collect from man whether he knows it or not. And they have grounds for what they do. And the judgment is a true judgment. And everything is ready for the meal (3:15-16)." I cannot imagine a more articulate statement of the system viewed whole than that statement of reward and punishment, foreknowledge and free will.

One. Defining the Human Condition: Abot

What guarantees the equity of God's governance therefore is that death is succeeded by life for those that merit it. "Don't give up hope of retribution" (1:7). "And do not have confidence in yourself until the day you die... And do not say, 'When I have time, I shall study,' for you may never have time" (2:4). "It's not your job to finish the work, but you're not free to walk away from it. If you have learned much Torah, they will give you a good reward. And your employer can be depended upon to pay your wages for what you do. And know what sort of reward is going to be given to the righteous in the coming time" (2:16). Reward and punishment are tempered by God's mercy and patience with human shortcomings: everything is in the effort.

The human situation portrayed by tractate Abot therefore entails alert and conscious conduct and imposes humility and fear. Man is a nullity, yet is an actor responsible for his own fate, has no reason to take pride in his condition, yet is subject to God's acute concern: "Reflect upon three things and you will not fall into the clutches of transgression: Know from whence you come, whither you are going, and before whom you are going to have to give a full account of yourself. From whence do you come? From a putrid drop. Whither are you going? To a place of dust, worms, and maggots And before whom are you going to give a full account of yourself? Before the King of kings of kings, the Holy One, blessed be he" (3:1).

So much for the reward for good conduct and the punishment for bad. The system portrayed in tractate Abot defines principles of virtue that register as good conduct. Of what does virtue consist? Since the human condition depends on God's will, virtue consists in making one's own wishes conform to those of God: "Make his wishes into your own wishes, so that he will make your wishes into his wishes. Put aside your wishes on account of his wishes, so that he will put aside the wishes of other people in favor of your wishes" (2:4). Those wishes are known, for God, in the Torah. Hence the supreme act of virtue consists in study of the Torah. Knowledge of God and the human condition derive from the act of grace comprised by the Torah, which informs man of what he otherwise could not have surmised, which is that he is created in the image of God; and which informs Israel that they are the children of God: "Precious is Adam, who was created in the image of God. It was an act of still greater love that it was made known to him that he was created in the image of God, as it is said, For in the image of God he made man (Gen. 9:6). Precious are Israelites, who are called children to the Omnipresent. It was an act of still greater love that they were called children to the Omnipresent, as it is said, You are the children of the Lord your God (Dt. 14:1). Precious are Israelites, to whom was given the precious thing. It was an act of still greater love that it was made known to them that to them was given that precious thing with which the world was made, as it is said, For I give you a good doctrine. Do not forsake my Torah (Prov. 4:2)" (3:14).

Torah-study forms the definition of the human vocation. Man was created to study the Torah: "If you have learned much Torah, do not puff yourself up on that account, for it was for that purpose that you were created" (2:8). That claim is hardly excessive, since through Torah-study man meets God: "If two sit together and between them do not pass teachings of Torah, lo, this is a seat of the scornful, as it is said, Nor sits in the seat of the scornful (Ps. 1:1). But two who are sitting, and words of Torah do pass between them — the Presence is with them, as it is said, Then they that feared the Lord spoke with one another, and the Lord hearkened and heard, and a book of remembrance was written before him, for them that feared the Lord and gave thought to His name (Mal. 3:16). I know that this applies to two. How do I know that even if a single person sits and works on Torah, the Holy One, blessed be he, sets aside a reward for him? As it is said, 'Let him sit alone and keep silent, because he had laid it upon him' (Lam. 3:28)." Torah-study is analogous to prayer, with this difference: when the Israelite prays, he talks to God, but when he studies, God talks to him.

Accordingly, God is present where the Torah is studied, and the way to know God is to study the Torah. "Three who ate at a single table and did not talk about teachings of Torah while at that table are as though they ate from dead sacrifices (Ps, 106:28), as it is said, For all tables are full of vomit and filthiness if they are without God (Ps. 106:28). But three who ate at a single table and did talk about teachings of Torah while at that table are as if they ate at the table of the Omnipresent, blessed is he, as it is said, 'And he said to me, This is the table that is before the Lord' (Ez. 41:22)" (3:2-3). So too the matter is elaborated: "Among ten who sit and work hard on Torah the Presence comes to rest, as it is said, 'God stands in the congregation of God' (Ps. 82:1). And how do we know that the same is so even of five? For it is said, 'And he has founded his group upon the earth' (Am. 9:6). And how do we know that this is so even of three? Since it is said, 'And he judges among the judges' (Ps. 82:1). And how do we know that this is so even of two? Because it is said, 'Then they that feared the Lord spoke with one another, and the Lord hearkened and heard' (Mal. 3:16). And how do we know that this is so even of one? Since it is said, 'In every place where I record my name I will come to you and I will bless you' (Ex. 20:24)" (3:6).

But study of Torah bears with it two further obligations. The first is to make a living. One cannot rely on Torah-learning to provide for material wealth. Second, one must carry out the teachings that one studies. "Fitting is learning in Torah along with a craft, for the labor put into the two of them makes one forget sin. And all learning of Torah which is not joined with labor is destined to be null and cause sin. And all who work with the community — let them work with them for the sake of Heaven. For the merit of their fathers strengthens them, and their fathers' righteousness stands forever. And as for you, I credit you with a great reward, as if you had done all of the work required by the community on your own merit alone" (2:2). But Torah-study should be ceaseless and not interrupted by extraneous thoughts: "He who is going along the way and repeating his Torah tradition but interrupts his repetition and says, 'How beautiful is that tree! How beautiful is that ploughed field!' — Scripture reckons it to him as if he has become liable for his life" (3:7). This implacable judgment shocks and has sustained the softening of interpretation: if one deems the beauty of the tree or field to interrupt the continuity of Torah-learning, so failing to perceive the lessons of the Torah contained within nature, then the penalty accrues. But read on its own, its message is clear: the stakes in Torah-learning are cosmic.

The temptation to concentrate on Torah-study to the exclusion of virtuous deeds provokes concern. Practice of the Torah's teachings, not merely mastery of their content, counts. What of the tension between knowing and doing, the outcome of Torah-study? The result of Torah-study is proper conduct, and without proper conduct Torah-study is null: "If there is no learning of Torah, there is no proper conduct. If there is no proper conduct, there is no learning in Torah. If there is no wisdom, there is no reverence. If there is no reverence, there is no wisdom If there is no understanding, there is no knowledge. If there is no knowledge, there is no understanding. If there is no sustenance, there is no Torah learning. If there is no Torah learning, there is no sustenance" (3:17). "He who learns so as to teach — they give him a chance to learn and to teach. He who learns so as to carry out his teachings — they give him a chance to learn, to teach, to keep, and to do" (4:5). Torah study yields this-worldly rewards: "Whoever keeps the Torah when poor will in the end keep it in wealth. And whoever treats the Torah as nothing when he is wealthy in the end will treat it as nothing in poverty. Keep your business to a minimum and make your business Torah. And be humble before everybody. And if you treat the Torah as nothing, you will have many treating you as nothing. And if you have labored in Torah, God has a great reward to give you" (4:9-10). But study of the Torah is its own reward and should not be construed as a source of benefit in this-worldly terms: "Do not make Torah teachings a crown with which to glorify yourself or a spade with which to dig. Whoever derives worldly benefit from teachings of Torah takes his life out of this world" (4:5).

To whom does the document speak? The "you" of the document is all Israel. But among Israelites, the document speaks most explicitly to masters and disciples, masters called upon to make decisions in courts as judges, disciples preparing through imitation of the masters for the same public responsibility. Abot is a handbook for judges, lawyers, and disciples. The lessons of Torah-study focus on the conduct of masters called upon to judge cases and dispense justice "Be prudent in judgment. Raise up many disciples. Make a fence for the Torah" (1:2). "Don't make yourself like one of those who make advocacy before judges while you yourself are judging a case. And when the litigants stand before you, regard them as guilty. And when they leave you, regard them as acquitted, when they have accepted your judgment." (1:8). "Examine the witnesses with great care. And watch what you say, lest they learn from what you say how to lie" (1:9). "Do not serve as a judge by yourself, for there is only One who serves as a judge all alone. And do not say, 'Accept my opinion.' For they have the choice in that matter, not you."

(4:8). "He who avoids serving as a judge breaks off the power of enmity, robbery, and false swearing. And he who is arrogant about making decisions is a fool, evil, and prideful" (4:7).

Israel seen whole, not merely the sector of judges, lawyers, and disciples, comes under consideration only generically. So far as the document sets forth a social philosophy, it covers the Temple, the Torah, and private acts of loving kindness (1:2). "On three things does the world stand: on justice, on truth, and on peace." "Love work. Hate authority. Don't get friendly with the government" (1:10). Virtue depends upon forming the right motivation for right action and invokes once more the issues of reward and punishment. "Do not be like servants who serve the master on condition of receiving a reward, but be like servants who serve the master not on condition of receiving a reward. And let the fear of Heaven be upon you" (1:3).

What doctrine of emotions emerges, defining the everyday outcome of virtue? The ideal Israelite accommodates, concedes, conciliates, gives way, forbears. Virtue requires perpetual patience, penitence and concern for the feelings and responses of others: "Let the respect owing to your fellow be as precious to you as the respect owing to you yourself. And don't be easy to anger. And repent one day before you die" (2:10). "The honor owing to your disciple should be as precious to you as yours. And the honor owing to your fellow should be like the reverence owing to your master. And the reverence owing to your master should be like the awe owing to Heaven" (4:12). One must not only forbear but actively conciliate his fellows: "Anyone from whom people take pleasure — the Omnipresent takes pleasure. And anyone from whom people do not take pleasure, the Omnipresent does not take pleasure" (3:10).

The right attitude then requires trembling and humility before God and man alike. Fear of sin is the key to virtuous conduct, even more than mastery of Torah-learning or wisdom: "For anyone whose fear of sin takes precedence over his wisdom, his wisdom will endure, And for anyone whose wisdom takes precedence over his fear of sin, his wisdom will not endure." Anyone whose deeds are more than his wisdom — his wisdom will endure. And anyone whose wisdom is more than his deeds — his wisdom will not endure" (3:9). Wisdom requires astuteness: "Who is a sage? He who learns from everybody. Who is strong? He who overcomes his desire. Who is rich? He who is happy in what he has. Who is honored? He who honors everybody" (4:1). "Do not despise anybody and do not treat anything as unlikely. For you have no one who does not have his time, and you have nothing which does not have its place" (4:3). So too, one must nurture the virtues of consideration and restraint: "Do not try to make amends with your fellow when he is angry, or comfort him when the corpse of his beloved is lying before him, or seek to find absolution for him at the moment at which he takes a vow, or attempt to see him when he is humiliated" (4:18).

Accordingly, a coherent message emerges from tractate Abot. It is in three parts. First, God is just and merciful, and those traits come to realization when

One. Defining the Human Condition: Abot

every individual answers to him for conduct in this life, with reward or punishment awaiting in the world to come. Virtue, second, consists in obedience to God's wishes, the upright person making his wishes conform to those of God. The requirements of virtue, third, are known in the Torah, the ultimate act of divine grace, which the Israelite is charged with mastering and carrying out.

II. TO WHOM, AND FOR WHOM, DOES THE DOCUMENT SPEAK? PROPOSITIONS AND PREOCCUPATIONS

The document speaks for Rabbinic sages and expresses their concerns. Its compilers and authors of its sayings conceive Israel to form not a corporate community bearing political power, e.g., to inflict acts of legitimate violence, but a collection of individuals, each responsible for himself before God. Israel is made up of persons possessed of the Torah and endowed with personal free will to obey or disobey the Torah. It is that endowment that defines the dynamics of the system put forth in the collected sayings. All Israelites enjoy the freedom to choose that originates with Adam and accounts for the disaster brought on by his deed: death above all. The Torah provides the antidote to death: access to eternal life. And each individual Israelite determines for himself his fate beyond the grave, everyone accorded a trial on his own. Accordingly that shift in Israel's circumstance from the public and the political to the private and the personal requires a shift in focus to the power of the individual to make his wishes and will conform to God's — a decision of a profoundly personal nature.

If, therefore, I had to select a single preoccupation paramount in the program of the document, I should turn to its account of virtue as submission to God and conciliation of one's fellow man. These traits of the submissive, humble, accommodating individual point to a persons lacking all political aspirations, deprived of this-worldly capacity to realize their own will. Collective action is not contemplated. The individual Israelite makes God's will his own will, in hope that God will make his will that of the Israelite.

What is striking is not only the absence of a collective, communal conception of Israel as a political entity but its attribution to God of the virtues of the vanquished. The system assigns to Heaven the operating program: justice and judgment, recompense and retribution. The reward of restraint lies in submission: the surrender of free will, which brings about sin, and the subordination of one's own will to God's. As Israel is subject to the nations in the here-and-now, so the Israelite accepts God's will and conforms to his commandments. The reward for the Israelites in the world to come proves commensurate. Then this world matters only as the antechamber of the world to come, and what makes a difference in the here and now is solely submission: acceptance of the givens of this world. The document, preoccupied with the individual and his parlous existence, in fact speaks to corporate Israel about its collective situation. What we have before us is a social philosophy rendered, paradoxically, in private and personal terms. All who aspire to live forever in affirming the eternity of their individuality comprise a moral collectivity, each individual knowing God in the same way as all the others, through the Torah.

III. Implicit Truths

The human condition portrayed by explicit statements in Abot yields the picture of humanity in God's image, Israel as God's first love — knowledge afforded to humanity and to Israel as an act of divine grace. But we gain little knowledge of the implicit truths of Abot by an act of mere recapitulation of these and other explicitly stated convictions. What is asserted is by definition an explicit affirmation, subject to contradiction, if not here, then in some other compilation. But my claim is to identify the givens of the document, what is implicit and taken as fact, never subjected to contrary contention or negotiation or revision. For that purpose we have to stand back and ask about the document as a whole.

What is affirmed by Abot is an encompassing system, not merely a mélange of episodic allegations. That system responds to the problem of evil that forms the dynamic of monotheist theology: how can God be conceived to be both all-powerful and just when the condition of humanity is contemplated: the righteous suffer, the wicked prosper, and exact justice prevails only sometimes. The solution to the problem of evil encompasses three aspects: [1] the fate of the individual in this life and after death, [2] the study of the Torah in response to the human condition, and [3] the nurture of virtue consequent upon Torah-study. [2] Study of the Torah leads to [3] virtue, which defines the righteous life worthy of eternity. The destiny of individuals is to die, with judgment and advent to the age to come for those that merit it. Study of the Torah invokes the presence of God. From Torah study the Israelite learns the lessons of the virtue that secures the world to come.

Implicit in the tripartite construction —Torah-study, virtue, resurrection — are norms of belief in principles so fundamental and generative that tractate Abot in all its specificity falls to pieces if any of these norms are defied. These norms define God, his character and conscience. The one, unique God who governs is just and merciful. That premise sustains the system. God is everywhere aware of what each individual in all of creation does at all times. Human beings, accordingly, live in an enchanted realm of the divine person's perpetual presence, subject to supervision yielding a detailed record of all their actions and attitudes. That record is examined when individuals die, with results that are articulated, as we have seen.

Before a single sentence in Abot can have been written, therefore, three convictions had to prevail. First, God, who forms a presence and a personality everywhere, is just, and God's rules of rationality pervade creation. Second, man is like God in possessing free will and is responsible for the choices that he makes. Third, the Torah forms the medium for the encounter with God in the world,

One. Defining the Human Condition: Abot

especially at meals. In that context, heresy consisted of three contrary convictions. There is no judge and there is no justice. Man is not subject to retribution for his actions. The Torah forms a tradition, an act of culture, but not the record of the words of the living God. What is implicit in Abot and therefore attested as norms of conviction is made explicit as heresy, a passage to which we shall return:

- A. All Israelites have a share in the world to come,
- B. as it is said, "your people also shall be all righteous, they shall inherit the land forever; the branch of my planting, the work of my hands, that I may be glorified" (Is. 60:21).
- C. And these are the ones who have no portion in the world to come:
- D. He who says, the resurrection of the dead is a teaching that does not derive from the Torah, and the Torah does not come from Heaven; and an Epicurean [who denies divine judgment and retribution].

Mishnah-tractate Sanhedrin 10:1

Here we find the Mishnah's explicit statements of the norms implicit in tractate Abot: resurrection, judgment, and the Torah, all in the form of heresies: denial of the Torah, of judgment, and therefore of resurrection as critical to the Torah's construction of human existence.

ENDNOTES

1 But see now Guenter Stemberger, "Mischna Avot. Fruehe Weisheitsschrift, pharisaeisches Erbe, oder spaetrabbinische Bildung?" *Zeitschrift der neutestamentliche Wissenschaft*, 2005.

2 I here reproduce my translation, *Torah from Our Sages: Pirke Avot. A New American Translation and Explanation*. Chappaqua, 1983: Rossel. Paperback edition: 1987. In print: S. Orange, 2005: Behrman House.

3 Contrast the view of Amram Tropper, *Wisdom, Politics, and Historiography. Tractate Avot in the Context of the Graeco-Roman Near East* (Oxford and New York, 2004: Oxford University Press). Tropper situates Abot in diverse and otherwise unconnected cultural settings and yields complete chaos.

2

The Categorical Structure of Knowledge: The Mishnah

I. The Document and its Program: Recurrent Questions

If we are able to concentrate on the contents of tractate Abot, it is because the tractate's sayings center on a few large subjects — no more than three fundamental ones — and set down coherent judgments upon them. But the Mishnah, a philosophical law code that came to closure at about 200 C.E., is not that way. It is topically diffuse, and it lays down judgments on a vast range of subjects, most of them involving this-worldly transactions.

The Mishnah is organized by subjects, sixty topical tractates in all, divided into six large divisions, with each subject systematically expounded in an orderly way. Implicit is only a miscellany of episodic propositions. Abstractions appear seldom, the evocative symbol, Torah, only occasionally, and reference to God rarely appears in the document. Resurrection of the dead and judgment occur in the passage cited at the end of Chapter One, and Torah-study makes an impact only alongside numerous other acts of virtue. The language is descriptive, not hortative, throughout. There is no summarizing the principal convictions of the document, no possibility of identifying the propositional premises of the various laws or even of their category-formations.

To specify the implicit convictions of the document requires a different approach altogether, one that concentrates on defining the prevailing modes of thought and analysis and their theological implications, rather than on what is implicit in theological affirmations as in tractate Abot. What makes it possible to speak of a program that governs this mass of information and to define premises that pervade the whole is not the topical organization but the recurrent questions that function throughout. Speaking about concrete topics, the Mishnah pursues a consistent program of analysis meant to demonstrate a few abstract principles. And when we understand what these are, we realize that the recurrent questions consistently produce proof of the unity of being, an ontology of monotheism.

The Mishnah's philosophy of classification aims at demonstrating the unity of all being: many things ascend to one thing, and one thing contains many things. At issue is to show when many things were really one thing (the many and the one, the species and the genus), and when one thing was really many things (the one and the many, the genus and the species). The Mishnah's is a system of hierarchical classification, showing that all things derive from one thing, one thing yields all things. Monotheism bears ontological consequences, and these are articulated case by case in the Mishnah's exposition of the law. "The many and the one" — how many things derive from a single source or form a single entity — defines a recurrent demonstration in the exposition of that law. The Mishnah's reflections on the unity of all being forms a massive exercise in which monotheism forms the implicit proposition. It is demonstrated that the unity of God is contained within nature and the norms of the social order — the two foci of the law of the Mishnah.

How this is accomplished in detail will emerge in a moment. First a few words of theory are in order. The system of ordering all things in proper place and under the proper rule and hierarchically maintains that like belongs with like and conforms to the rule governing like, the unlike goes over to the opposite and conforms to the opposite rule — analogical-contrastive analysis. The mode of thought is that of natural philosophy, out of which natural science has evolved. That is to say, faced with a mass of facts, we are able [1] to bring order — that is to say, to determine the nature of things — by finding out which items resemble others and, [2] determining the taxic indicator that forms of the lot a single classification, and then [3] determining the single rule to which all cases conform.

That method of bringing structure and order out of the chaos of indeterminate facts pertains, on the very surface, to persons, places, things; to actions and attitudes; to the natural world of animals, minerals, vegetables, the social world of castes and peoples, actions and functions, and the supernatural world of the holy and the unclean, the possession of Heaven and the possession of earth, the sanctified and the common. Many things can be shown, through proper classification, comparison and contrast of pertinent traits, to be one thing. And all things merge in the hierarchy of being that one thing comprises. The whole depends upon three premises: [1] the importance of comparison and contrast, with the supposition that [2] like follows the like, and the unlike follows the opposite, rule; and [3] when we classify, we also hierarchize, which yields the argument from hierarchical classification: if this, which is the lesser, follows rule X, then that, which is the greater, surely should follow rule X.

The telos of thought in the Mishnah, accordingly, is such that many things are made to say one thing, which concerns the nature of being. So the Mishnah's system must be deemed ontological. For it is a statement of an ontological order that the document's system makes when it claims that all things are not only orderly, but ordered in such wise that many things fall into one classification, and one thing may hold together many things of a diverse classifications. These two matched propositions — many things are one, one thing encompasses many — complement each other, because, in forming matched opposites, the two provide a single, complete and final judgment of the whole of being, social, natural, supernatural alike. The issue, however, concerns nature, not supernature, and sifts the everyday data of the here and the now. It is we who connect the results of the repeated demonstrations with theological premises of monotheism.

Let us turn to concrete illustrations of these abstract exercises. One of the most interesting demonstrations is the analysis of the several taxa into which a single action may fall, with an account of the multiple consequences, e.g., as to sanctions that are called into play, for a single action. The right taxonomy of persons, actions, and things will show the unity of all being by finding many things in one thing, and that forms the first of the two components of what I take to be the philosophy's teleology.

MISHNAH-TRACTATE KERITOT 3:9

A. There is one who ploughs a single furrow and is liable on eight counts of violating a negative commandment:
B. [specifically, it is] he who (1) ploughs with an ox and an ass [Deut. 22:10], which are (2,3) both Holy Things, in the case of (4) [ploughing] Mixed Seeds in a vineyard [Deut. 22:9], (5) in the Seventh Year [Lev. 25:4], (6) on a festival [Lev. 23:7] and who was both a (7) priest [Lev. 21:1] and (8) a Nazirite [Num. 6:6] [ploughing] in a grave-yard.
C. Hanania b. Hakhinai says, "Also: He is [ploughing while] wearing a garment of diverse kinds" [Lev. 19:19, Deut. 22:11).
D. They said to him, "This is not within the same class."
E. He said to them, "Also the Nazir [B8] is not within the same class [as the other transgressions]."

Here is a case in which more than a single set of flogging is called for. B's felon is liable to 312 stripes, on the listed counts. The ox is sanctified to the altar, the ass to the Temple upkeep (B2,3). Hanania's contribution is rejected since it has nothing to do with ploughing, and sages' position is equally flawed. The main point, for our inquiry, is simple. The one action draws in its wake multiple consequences. Classifying a single thing as a mixture of many things then forms a part of the larger intellectual address to the nature of mixtures. But it yields a result that, in the analysis of an action, far transcends the metaphysical problem of mixtures, because it moves us toward the ontological solution of the unity of being.

If then many things become one thing, how about the one thing that yields the many? If we can show that a single classification may be *subdivided*, then the unity of the many in the one is demonstrated from a fresh angle. If so, the systemic contention concerning the fundamental and essential unity of all being finds reinforcement. That the question is faced may be shown, as usual in so coherent a piece of writing as the Mishnah, at a variety of passages. One is as follows:

MISHNAH-TRACTATE NAZIR 6:4-5

6:4 A. A Nazir who was drinking wine all day long is liable only on one count.
   B. [If] they said to him, "Don't drink it!" "Don't drink it!" and he continues drinking, he is liable on each and every count [of drinking].
   C. [If] he was cutting his hair all day long, he is liable only on a single count.
   D. [If] they said to him, "Don't cut it!" "Don't cut it!" and he continued to cut his hair, he is liable for each and every count [of cutting].
   E. [If] he was contracting corpse uncleanness all day long, he is liable on only one count.
   F. If they said to him, "Don't contract corpse uncleanness!" "Don't contract corpse uncleanness!" and he continued to contract corpse uncleanness, he is liable for each and every count.

6:5 A. Three things are prohibited to a Nazir: [corpse] uncleanness, cutting the hair, and anything which goes forth from the grapevine.
   B. A more strict rule applies to corpse uncleanness and haircutting than applies to that which comes forth from the grapevine.
   C. For corpse uncleanness and haircutting cause the loss of the days already observed, but [violating the prohibition against] that which goes forth from the vine does not cause the loss of the days already observed.
   D. A more strict rule applies to that which goes forth from the vine than applies to corpse uncleanness and haircutting.
   E. For that which goes forth from the vine allows for no exception, but corpse uncleanness and haircutting allow for exceptions,
   F. in the case of [cutting the hair for] a religious duty and in the case of finding a neglected corpse [with no one else to provide for burial, in which case, the Nazir is absolutely required to bury the corpse].
   G. A more strict rule applies to corpse uncleanness than to haircutting.
   H. For corpse uncleanness causes the loss of all the days previously observed and imposes the liability for an offering.
   I. But haircutting causes the loss of only thirty days and does not impose liability for an offering.

At M. Naz. 6:4 we take up the issue of disjoined actions, for each of which one is liable, when these actions are of a single species. What distinguishes one action from another, when all are of the same species, is that one is made aware each time he does the prohibited action that he is forbidden to do so. Then each action is individual. But if not, then all of the actions form a single sustained action, for which one is liable on only one count. This interesting conception then imposes upon the differentiation of actions the consideration of intentionality: the man now knows that the particular action he is about to undertake is prohibited. Hence it seems to me a case in which we invoke intentionality in the work of the classification of actions (=counts of culpability). What is at stake in the issue? It is the application

Two. The Categorical Structure of Knowledge: The Mishnah

of hierarchical classification, which as we know forms the goal of the philosophy's method of classification. So we see the unity of philosophical medium and philosophical message. For M. Naz. 6:5 takes the facts of Scripture and forms of them a composition of hierarchical classification, in which the taxic indicators are laid out in accord with a single program.

I have repeatedly claimed that the recognition that one thing becomes many does not challenge the philosophy of the unity of all being, but confirms the main point. Why do I insist on that proposition? The reason is simple. If we can show that differentiation flows from within what is differentiated, — that is, from the intrinsic or inherent traits of things — then we confirm that at the heart of things is a fundamental ontological being, single, cogent, simple, that is capable of diversification, yielding complexity and diversity. The upshot is to be stated with emphasis. *That diversity in species or diversification in actions follows orderly lines confirms the claim that there is that single point from which many lines come forth.* Carried out in proper order — [1] the many form one thing, and [2] one thing yields many — the demonstration then leaves no doubt as to the truth of the matter. Ideally, therefore, we shall argue from the simple to the complex, showing that the one yields the many, one thing, many things, two, four.

MISHNAH-TRACTATE SHABBAT 1:1

1:1   A.   [Acts of] transporting objects from one domain to another, [which violate] the Sabbath, (1) are two, which [indeed] are four [for one who is] inside, (2) and two which are four [for one who is] outside,
- B. How so?
- C. [If on the Sabbath] the beggar stands outside and the householder inside,
- D. [and] the beggar stuck his hand inside and put [a beggar's bowl] into the hand of the householder,
- E. or if he took [something] from inside it and brought it out,
- F. the beggar is liable, the householder is exempt.
- G. [If] the householder stuck his hand outside and put [something] into the hand of the beggar,
- H. or if he took [something] from it and brought it inside,
- I. the householder is liable, and the beggar is exempt.
- J. [If] the beggar stuck his hand inside, and the householder took [something] from it,
- K. or if [the householder] put something in it and he [the beggar] removed
- L. both of them are exempt.
- M. [If] the householder put his hand outside and the beggar took [something] from it,
- N. or if [the beggar] put something into it and [the householder] brought it back inside,
- O. both of them are exempt.

M. Shab. 1:1 classifies diverse circumstances of transporting objects from private to public domain. The purpose is to assess the rules that classify as culpable or exempt from culpability diverse arrangements. The operative point is that a prohibited action is culpable only if one and the same person commits the whole of the violation of the law. If two or more people share in the single action, neither of them is subject to punishment. At stake therefore is the conception that one thing may be many things, and if that is the case, then culpability is not incurred by any one actor.

The consequence of showing that one thing is many things is set forth with great clarity in the consideration not of the actor but of the action. One class of actions is formed by those that violate the sanctity of the Sabbath. Do these form many subdivisions, and, if so, what difference does it make? Here is a famous passage that shows how a single class of actions yields multiple and complex speciation, while remaining one:

MISHNAH-TRACTATE SHABBAT 7:1-2

7:1 A. A general rule did they state concerning the Sabbath:
  B. Whoever forgets the basic principle of the Sabbath and performed many acts of labor on many different Sabbath days is liable only for a single sin offering.
  C. He who knows the principle of the Sabbath and performed many acts of labor on many different Sabbaths is liable for the violation of each and every Sabbath.
  D. He who knows that it is the Sabbath and performed many acts of labor on many different Sabbaths is liable for the violation of each and every generative category of labor.
  E. He who performs many acts of labor of a single type is liable only for a single sin offering.

7:2 A. The generative categories of acts of labor [prohibited on the Sabbath] are forty less one:
  B. (1) he who sews, (2) ploughs, (3) reaps, (4) binds sheaves, (5) threshes, (6) winnows, (7) selects [fit from unfit produce or crops], (8) grinds, (9) sifts, (10) kneads, (11) bakes;
  C. (12) he who shears wool, (13) washes it, (14) beats it, (15) dyes it;
  D. (16) spins, (17) weaves,
  E. (18) makes two loops, (19) weaves two threads, (20) separates two threads;
  F. (21) ties, (22) unties,
  G. (23) sews two stitches, (24) tears in order to sew two stitches;
  H. (25) he who traps a deer, (26) slaughters it, (27) flays it, (28) salts it, (29) cures its hide, (30) scrapes it, and (31) cuts it up;
  I. (32) he who writes two letters, (33) erases two letters in order to write two letters;
  J. (34) he who builds, (35) tears down;
  K. (36) he who puts out a fire, (37) kindles a fire;

Two. *The Categorical Structure of Knowledge: The Mishnah* 17

L. (38) he who hits with a hammer; (39) he who transports an object from one domain to another —
M. lo, these are the forty generative acts of labor less one.

Now we see how the fact that one thing yields many things confirms the philosophy of the unity of all being. For the many things all really are one thing, here, the intrusion into sacred time of actions that do not belong there. M. Shab. 7:1-2 presents a parallel to the discussion of how many things can be shown to be one thing and to fall under a single rule, and how one thing may be shown to be many things and to invoke multiple consequences. It is that interest at M. 7:1 which accounts for the inclusion of M. 7:2, and the exposition of M. 7:2 occupies much of the tractate that follows. Along these same lines in Mishnah-tractate Sanhedrin the specification of the many and diverse sins or felonies that are penalized in a given way shows us how many things are one thing — belong in a single category-formation, there pertaining to the form of the death penalty that pertains — and then draws in its wake the specification of those many things, so here we find a similar exercise. It is one of classification, working in two ways, then: the power of a unifying taxon, the force of a differentiating and divisive one. The list of the acts of labor then gives us the categories of work, and performing any one of these constitutes a single action in violation of the Sabbath.

How, exactly, do these things work themselves out? If one does not know that the Sabbath is incumbent upon him, then whatever he does falls into a single taxon. If he knows that the Sabbath exists and violates several Sabbath days in succession, what he does falls into another taxon. If one knows that the Sabbath exists in principle and violates it in diverse ways, e.g., through different types of prohibited acts of labor, then many things become still more differentiated. The consideration throughout, then, is how to assess whether something is a single or multiple action as to the reckoning of the consequence.

II. TO WHOM, AND FOR WHOM, DOES THE DOCUMENT SPEAK? PROPOSITIONS AND PREOCCUPATIONS

The principal proposition of the Mishnah, concerning the ontological unity of being, with many things forming one thing, and one thing yielding many things, proves entirely congruent with one important conception of Middle Platonism, neo-Platonism, and Plotinus, concerning the unity of all being. The Mishnah's paramount proposition runs along the lines of important fundamentals of the philosophy that came to full expression in the writings of Plotinus (204-270) in the name of Plato, and to that message we have now to turn.[1] Bréhier states the matter in the simplest possible way:

> ...the universe appears as a series of forms each of which depends hierarchically on the preceding, and the universe can be the object of rational thought.[2]

Let us begin with the most difficult point, deriving from a general description of Middle, or Neo-Platonism, the focus on the unity of being, from the tangible to the intangible. Bréhier states:

> We can conceive of a unity that increases to the point where the parts of a being fuse and become almost inseparable. For instance, we cannot speak in the same sense of the parts of a living body and of the parts of a science; in a living body the parts are solidary but are locally separated, whereas in a science a part is a theorem and each theorem contains potentially every other theorem. Thus we see how an additional degree of unification takes us from the corporeal to the spiritual.[3]

Here we see, in abstraction, considerations that we locate in very concrete terms in the progress from classification of things to their hierarchization and finally to their unification, shown in the fact that as one thing is made up of — holds together in unity — many things, so many things emerge from one thing. And that, in abstract language, forms the centerpiece of the Mishnaic interest in classification.

So too, as Bréhier says, "But every imperfect reality or union of parts implies a more complete unity beyond itself...In the absence of the higher unity, everything disperses, crumbles and loses its being. Nothing is other than through the One." As to method, what is at hand is "explaining a particular aspect of reality by relating it to a more perfect unity." What we find in the Mishnah is the distinctive definition of those components of reality that are to be taken up in the quest for ontological unity: the this and that of the every day and the here and now.

Specifically, Plotinus in the name of Plato[4] set forth a doctrine of the hierarchical order of being, in which many things are subsumed within one thing, and one thing yields many things, from the lowest order, which is diverse, to the highest, which is unified. The doctrine of the One in Plotinus may be best summarized as follows:

> The One is infinite, the others finite; the One is creator, the others creatures; the One is entirely itself, entirely infinite, the others are both finite and infinite...the One has no otherness, the others are other than the One. It is not the case that while the Forms exist, the One does not. Rather the One exists in an infinite way, the others finitely....[5]

The centerpiece of the system then is the conception of the One, and the fundamental hierarchical unity of being in the orderly world that descends from the One.

Accordingly, moving from Aristotle to neo-Platonism opens the way to the rough and ready comparison between the philosophical message of a critical and paramount philosophical system, that which came to full expression only after the closure of the Mishnah, with Plotinus in the middle of the third century, and the

Two. The Categorical Structure of Knowledge: The Mishnah

philosophical message of the Mishnah, at the end of the second century or beginning of the third.

Let me proceed with a simple definition of "Platonism and neo-Platonism," that supplied by A. H. Armstrong, as follows (with the pertinent points I wish to emphasize given in italics, supplied by me):

> Neoplatonism, the form of Platonism developed by Plotinus in the third century A.D., contains among its leading ideas the following:
> 1. There is plurality of spheres of being, arranged in hierarchical descending order, the last and lowest comprising the universe, which exists in time and space and is perceptible to the senses.
> 2. Each sphere of being is derive from its superior, a derivation that is not a process in time or space.
> 3. Each derived being is established in its own reality by turning back toward its superior in a movement of contemplative desire, which is implicit in the original creative impulse of outgoing that it receives from its superior....
> 4. Each sphere of being is an image or expression on a lower level of the sphere above it.
> 5. Degrees of being are also degrees of unity; in each subsequent sphere of being there is greater multiplicity, more separateness, and increasing limitation, — till the atomic individualization of the spatiotemporal world is reached.
> 6. The supreme sphere of being, and through it all of what in any sense exists, derives from the ultimate principle, which is absolutely free from determinations and limitations and utterly transcends any conceivable reality, so that it may be said to be 'beong being.' As it has no limitations, so it has no division, attributes, or qualifications; it cannot really be named but may be called 'the One' to designate its complete simplicity. It may also be called 'the Good' as the source of all perfections and the ultimate goal of return; for the impulse of outgoing and return that constitutes the hierarchy of derived reality comes from and leads back to the Good.
> 7. Since this supreme principle is absolutely simple and undetermined (or devoid of specific traits), man's knowledge of it must be radically different from any other kind of knowledge: it is not an object (a separate, determined, limited thing) and no predicates can be applied to it; hence it can be known only if it raises the mind to an immediate union with itself, which cannot be imagined or described. [6]

The point at which I find an important common proposition is the conviction of a hierarchical order of being, in which, as one ascends, one moves ever toward a more unified realm of being.

This conception here is expressed in the reverse order: as one descends, things become more complex, so the one yields the many. I see no fundamental difference between the two positions on the unity of being and subordinated matters I should classify as ontological. Armstrong's points 1 and 5 thus appear to me to coincide with the Mishnah's fundamental and repeatedly demonstrated proposition about the unity of being, attained through the hierarchical classification of all things.

It is the proposition of the One that matters; the basic point serves our purpose full well: the first aspect of the One is "as conclusion of the metaphysical and religious search for a primary reality which can act as explanation of the universe." The One is transcendent and absolute. The One is "not only self-thinking but self-willing and self-loving." At stake is the proposition that "above this multiple unity, which constitutes the intelligible world, we must posit...the absolute One without distinction and without variety."[7] Bréhier shows the kindred spirit of the two philosophies, Plotinus's and the Mishnah's:

> To think, for Plotinus, is then to comprehend the unity of a composition of which sensations acquaint us only with the dispersed elements — the intention of the dancer in the multiplicity of movements in a dance figure, the living unity of the circular course of a star across the infinity of positions it occupies successively. It is to proceed toward a reality which, from losing anything of the richness of sensation, quite to the contrary goes beyond it and uncovers its depth.[8]

The metaphor of the dance captures the whole. Here, I would claim, the Judaic philosophers would indeed concur even in detail. They express the counterpart to the multiplicity of movements in a dance figure, the infinity of positions the star occupies. And then, in the detail, they recover not intention but rule, not circular course but the laws of motion.

If as I claim the Mishnah sets forth a system that philosophers of the day properly instructed can have identified as philosophical in method and message, if (obviously) not in medium, then we must ask ourselves, *Cui bono*? Or more precisely, not to whose advantage, but rather, *against* whose position, did the Judaic philosophical system adumbrated by the Mishnah then propose to argue? When we realize that at stake is a particular means for demonstrating the unity of God, we readily identify as the principal focus the pagan reading of the revealed world of the here and the now, and, it must follow, the Mishnah as a philosophy stood over against the pagan philosophy of the world of its time and place.

The fundamental argument in favor of the unity of God in the philosophy of the Mishnah is by showing the hierarchical order, therefore the unity, of the data of the social and natural world. The created world therefore is made to testify to the unity of being, and — to say the obvious with very heavy emphasis — *the power of the philosophy derives from its capacity for hierarchical classification.*

Some elementary comparisons of the Judaic, Christian, and pagan systems of Middle Platonism seem to me made possible, in a very preliminary way to be sure, by Armstrong:

Two. The Categorical Structure of Knowledge: The Mishnah

> The difference here between pagans and Christians...is a difference about the degree of religious relevance of the material cosmos, and, closely connected with this, about the relative importance of general, natural, and special, supernatural, divine self-manifestation and self-communication. On the one side, the pagan, there is the conviction that a multiple self-communication and self-revelation of divinity takes place always and everywhere in the world, and that good and wise men everywhere...have been able to find the way to God and the truth about God in and through rational reflection on themselves and on the world, not only the heavens but the earth, and the living unity of the whole. On the other side, the Christian, there is indeed a readiness to see the goodness and beauty of the visible cosmos as a testimony to God's creation...but the religious emphasis lies elsewhere. Saving truth and the self-communication of the life of God come through the Incarnation of God as a man and through the human...society of which the God-Man is the head, the Church...It is only in the Church that material things become means of revelation and salvation through being understood in the light of Scripture and Church tradition and used by God's human ministers in the celebration of the Church's sacraments. It is the ecclesiastical cosmos, not the natural cosmos, which appears to be of primary religious importance for the Christian.[9]

If God is revealed in the artifacts of the world, then, so pagans in general considered, God must be multiple. No, the philosophy of the Mishnah is here seen to respond. Here we find a Judaic argument, within the premises of paganism, against paganism. To state with emphasis what I conceive to be that argument:

the very artifacts that appear *multiple in fact form classes of things, and, moreover, these classes themselves are subject to a reasoned ordering, by appeal to this-worldly characteristics signified by properties and indicative traits.*

Monotheism hence is to be demonstrated by appeal to those very same data that for paganism prove the opposite. The medium of hierarchical classification, which is Aristotle's, conveys the message of the unity of being, which is Plato's and Plotinus's, in the this-worldly mode of discourse formed by the framers of the Mishnah. The way to one God, ground of being and ontological unity of the world, lies through "rational reflection on themselves and on the world," this world, which yields a living unity encompassing the whole. That claim, conducted in an argument covering overwhelming detail in the Mishnah, directly faces the issue as framed by paganism. Immanent in its medium, it is transcendent in its message. And I hardly need spell out the simple reasons, self-evident in Armstrong's words, for dismissing as irrelevant to their interests the Christian reading of the cosmos. To the Mishnah's sages, it is not (merely) wrong, it is insufficient.

And yet, that is not the whole story. For the Mishnah's sages reach into Scripture for their generative categories, and, in doing so, they address head-on a Christianity that Armstrong centers, with entire soundness, upon the life of the

Church of Jesus Christ, God-Man. We do well here to review Armstrong's language: "It is only in the Church that material things become means of revelation and salvation through being understood in the light of Scripture and Church tradition and used by God's human ministers in the celebration of the Church's sacraments."

The framers of the Mishnah will have responded, *"It is in the Torah that material things are identified and set forth as a means of revelation."*

Again Armstrong: "It is the ecclesiastical cosmos, not the natural cosmos, which appears to be of primary religious importance for the Christian."

To this the philosophers responsible for the system set forth in the Mishnah reply, *"It is the scriptural account of the cosmos that forms our generative categories, which, by the power of intellect, we show to constitute an ordered, hierarchical unity of being."*

So the power of this identification of "the ecclesiastical cosmos" is revealed when we frame the cosmos of the Mishnah by appeal to its persistent response to the classifications and categories of Scripture. If the Church as Armstrong portrays matters worked out an ecclesiastical cosmos, only later on producing the Bible as it did, for its part the philosophy of the Mishnah framed a scriptural cosmos, — and then read it philosophically in the way in which I have explained matters. We may therefore identify three distinct positions on the reading of the natural world: the pagan, the Christian, and the Judaic. The one reads nature as a source of revelation. The other two insist on a medium of mediation between nature and intellect. For Christianity it is, as Armstrong says, ecclesiastical, and, as I claim, for the Mishnah, the medium of mediation of nature lies through revelation, the Torah.

Given their circumstance, the philosophers' search, for the many things that they would show are really one, in Scripture's entire practical program, as worked out in Exodus, Leviticus, Numbers, and Deuteronomy, is not only indicative. By not merely appealing to the authority of Scripture, but by themselves analyzing the revealed truths of Scripture, the intellects of the Mishnah accomplished their purposes. By themselves showing the order and unity inherent within Scripture's list of topics, the philosophers on their own power meant to penetrate into the ground of being as God has revealed matters. This they did by working their way back from the epiphenomena of creation to the phenomenon of Creation — then to the numinous, that is, the Creator. That self-assigned challenge forms an intellectual vocation worthy of a particular kind of philosopher, an Israelite one. And, in my view, it explains also why in the Mishnah philosophers produced their philosophy in the form that they chose.

III. Implicit Truths

Showing that all things can be ordered, and that all orders can be set into relationship with one another, we transform method into message. The principal message of the Mishnah's enterprise — that of hierarchical classification — is that many things really form a single thing, the many species a single genus, the many genera an encompassing and well-crafted, cogent whole. Every time we speciate, as we do in nearly every chapter of the Mishnah, we affirm that proposition. Each successful labor of forming relationships among species, e.g., making them into a genus, or identifying the hierarchy of the species, proves it again. Not only so, but when we can show that many things are really one, or that one thing yields many (the reverse and confirmation of the former), we say in a fresh way a single immutable truth, the one of this philosophy concerning the unity of all being in an orderly composition of all things within a single taxon. Exegesis always is repetitive — and a sound exegesis of the systemic exegesis must then be equally so, everywhere explaining the same thing in the same way.

The species point to the genus, all classes to one class, all taxa properly hierarchized then rise to the top of the structure and the system forming one taxon. So all things ascend to, reach one thing. All that remains is for the theologian to define that one thing: God — God in the form, God in the order, God in the structure, God in the heights, God at the head of the great chain of well-ordered being, in the proper hierarchy. True, God in his perfect unity is premise, scarcely mentioned. But it is because God's name does not have to be mentioned when the whole of the order of being says that name, and only that name, and always that name, the Name unspoken because it is always in the echo, the silent, thin voice, the numinous in all phenomena of relationship: the truly unified, single and singular God of the Mishnah's obsessive demonstrations.

ENDNOTES

[1] On Middle Platonism and Plotinus I consulted the following works:
Armstrong, A. Hilary, *Plotinian and Christian Studies* (London, 1979: Variorum Reprints).
Armstrong, A. H., *The Architecture of the Intelligible Universe in the Philosophy of Plotinus. An Analytical and Historical Study* (Amsterdam, 1967: Adolf M. Hakkert, Publisher).
Bréhier, Émile, *The Philosophy of Plotinus*. Translated by Joseph Thomas (Chicago, 1958: University of Chicago Press).
Dillon, J. M., and A. A. Long, *The Question of "Eclecticism." Studies in Later Greek Philosophy* (Los Angeles and Berkeley, 1988: University of California Press).
Katz, Joseph, *The Philosophy of Plotinus. Representative Books from the Enneads. Selected and Translated with an Introduction* (N.Y., 1950: Appleton-Century-Crofts, Inc.)
O'Brien, Elmer, *The Essential Plotinus. Representative Treatises from the Enneads* (Repr., 1975: Hackett Publishing Co., Inc.)
Rist, J. M., *Plotinus: The Road to Reality* (Cambridge, 1967: Cambridge University Press).
Sambursky, Samuel, *The Concept of Place in Late Neoplatonism* (Jerusalem, 1982: Israel Academy of Arts and Sciences).
Sambursky, Samuel, and S. Pines, *The Concept of Time in Late Neoplatonism* (Jerusalem, 1971: Israel Academy of Arts and Sciences).

Turnbull, Grace H., *The Essence of Plotinus. Extracts from the Six Enneads and Porphyry's Life of Plotinus*. Based on the Translation by Stephen Mackenna. (N.Y., 1948: Oxford University Press).

[2] Bréhier, *Plotinus*, p. 43

[3] Émile Bréhier, *The History of Philosophy. The Hellenistic and Roman Age* (Chicago and London, 1965: The University of Chicago Press). Translated by Wade Baskin,

[4] My argument has no bearing on the relationship between Plato and Middle Platonism in general, or Plotinus in particular. On this matter I read "Elements in the Thought of Plotinus at Variance with Classical Intellectualism," Armstrong, A. Hilary, *Plotinian and Christian Studies* (London, 1979: Variorum Reprints), paper XVI.

[5,6] J. M. Rist, *Plotinus: The Road to Reality* (Cambridge, 1967: Cambridge University Press), p. 37.

[7] Armstrong, A. H., "Platoism and Neoplatonism," *Encyclopaedia Britannica* (Chicago, 1975) 14:539-545

[8] ibid., p. 45.

[9] ibid., p. 11.

[10] "Man in the Cosmos," Armstrong, A. Hilary, *Plotinian and Christian Studies* (London, 1979: Variorum Reprints) No. XVII, p. 11,

3

The Laws of Intellect: Sifra

I. THE DOCUMENT AND ITS PROGRAM: RECURRENT QUESTIONS

The premise of Sifra is that the Torah contains God's words in God's own wording and so affords access to God's mind: how he thinks as much as what he says. Accordingly revelation takes place in the logic of the grammar that animates the words of the Torah, not only in the category-formations that govern in nature and society, the topics that cohere. That premise intersected with, and contradicted, the one of the Mishnah.

The Mishnah had yielded an account of creation that appealed to systematic hierarchical classification to yield ontological monotheism: proof from the character of creation that all things rise to one thing, one thing serves as source for all things, diversity gives way to unit, simplicity to complexity. The Mishnah thus derived category-formations from the traits of nature and the social order, with shared this-worldly traits signaling a rule common to a given classification of things.

But Sifra called into question the possibility of proving from traits of the natural and social orders the unity of all being. The challenge lay in the repeated demonstration in Sifra that category-formation based on this-worldly traits does not produce incontrovertible results. There is always a further distinction to be made among supposedly uniform data, always a weak point in the hierarchization of classifications. But Scripture, the Torah, provides what the natural and social orders cannot. Nature and the order of society do not afford access to the logic of creation, only the Torah does, and the very language of the Torah affords access to God's logic in creation.

In Sifra, a verse-by-verse commentary to the book of Leviticus, ca. 300 C.E., we therefore find a powerful critique of the Mishnah's this-worldly view of the principles of category-formation. The authorship of Sifra set forth its critique when it cited verbatim passages of the Mishnah and repeatedly criticized the Mishnah's mode of classification by appeal to the traits of things. In that authorship's view expressed in case after case the correct classification of things is dictated only by Scripture. Logic that appeals to intrinsic traits, ignoring the classifications dictated by Scripture, is flawed and unreliable. This other principle of the logical classification of things appeals to a received and not an intrinsic mode of classification. Specifically, it is *Scripture's* classifications, and not those inherent in things by their very nature, that alone serves to dictate how we make our lists and so derive our general principles. The implicit norm set forth by Sifra thus maintained that the Torah provided the key to the divine intellect, comparable to the Mishnah's implicit norm that this world, properly analyzed in hierarchical classification of worldly data, expressed the perfect unity of God.

The Mishnah thus was focused on the character of creation, invoking the principles of natural history. Sifra was centered on character of revelation, leveling a critique at the sufficiency of creation to yield truth when not illuminated by revelation. The premise of Sifra accordingly concerns itself with the same problem that preoccupied the framers of the Mishnah, the organization and purpose of knowledge. The Mishnah appealed to the traits of things to turn facts into propositions. It employed topical category-formations to organize data into intelligible constructions. These category-formations took shape around free-standing subjects, e.g., vows, blessings, the Sabbath, and not around the exegesis of Scripture. That is why proof-texts drawn from Scripture in support of topical propositions, e.g., of hierarchical classification, prove rare in the Mishnah, which stands on its own foundations of analogical-contrastive analysis. Sifra's framers took a very different approach to the organization and articulation of knowledge, according priority to the category-formations of Scripture, its mode of organizing data, over those defined by the traits of things. And the Mishnah thus left open the question of its own standing vis-à-vis Scripture, rarely citing proof-texts for its propositions. Sifra, by contrast, insisted that Scripture is the sole source of reliable rules of classification. That is its premise and its recurrent, implicit proposition, as we shall see.

The premise of Sifra's framers thus maintained that Scripture reveals not only God's wishes but God's actual words, the modes of thought and analysis that govern in God's mind: the vocabulary, grammar, and syntax of God's own intellect. When we know the principles of logical structure and especially those of hierarchical classification that animate the Torah, we can undertake part of the task of expansion and amplification, that is, join in the processes of thought that, in the mind of God, yielded the Torah. For when we know how God thought in giving the Torah to Moses at Sinai and so accounting for the classifications and their ordering in the very creation of the world, we can ourselves enter into the Torah and participate in its processes.

Sifra takes for granted the outcome of the Mishnah and is comprehensible only in its dialogue with the Mishnah. For Sifra's authorship conducts a sustained polemic against the failure of the Mishnah to cite Scripture very much or systematically to link its ideas to Scripture through the medium of formal

Three. The Laws of Intellect: Sifra

demonstration by exegesis. Sifra's rhetorical exegesis follows a standard redactional form. Scripture will be cited. Then a statement will be made about its meaning, or a statement of law correlative to that Scripture will be given. That statement sometimes cites the Mishnah, often verbatim. Finally, the author of Sifra invariably states, "Now is that not (merely) logical?" And the point of that statement will be, Can this position not be gained through the working of mere logic, based upon facts supplied (to be sure) by Scripture? Here is a simple statement of the matter:

Sifra III:IX.

1 A. When Scripture states, "...from the herd," it serves an exclusionary purpose, namely to exclude a beast suffering a terminal ailment. [Such a beast may not be offered on the altar.]
B. Is that not a matter of a logical inference?
C. Namely, If a blemished beast, which is permitted for use for ordinary food, is unfit for use on the altar, a beast suffering a terminal ailment, which is forbidden for use for ordinary food, surely should be unfit for use on the altar.
D. [No, that reasoning does not apply at all, for lo:] forbidden fat and blood will prove to the contrary, for they are forbidden for use as ordinary food, but they are most certainly valid for use on the altar [where they are to be burned up]!
E. No, if you have stated that rule in the case of forbidden fat and blood, which derive from something that, under ordinary circumstances, is permitted [for use as food, for one may eat fat and make use of blood of a valid beast[, will you say the same of the beast suffering from a terminal ailment, the whole of which is forbidden for use on the altar? [So the logical demonstration is a good one, and a verse of Scripture is needless to make the point.]
F. A fowl that has been strangled [as an offering [will prove to the contrary, for the whole of it is forbidden [for ordinary food[yet [by definition[is valid for use on the altar.
G. No, if you have invoked the case of fowl that has been strangled, it is the very fact that it has been sanctified that renders it forbidden for ordinary use.
H. But will you say the same of a beast suffering a terminal ailment, which is not forbidden by reason of its having been sanctified? Since it is prohibited for reasons other than its having been sanctified, it should not be declared unfit for use on the altar!
I. Lo, there is your answer to the proof [and there is no argument a fortiori to be made].
J. Thus when Scripture states, "...from the herd," it serves an exclusionary purpose, namely to exclude a beast suffering a terminal ailment. [Such a beast may not be offered on the altar.]

The key language comes at B: Scripture's statement is not required, since logic can have yielded the same point. But the exposition keeps turning up exceptions to the rule proposed as logical. The upshot is, logic on its own does not yield reliable results.

The polemical power of Sifra lies in its repetitive demonstration that the stated position, citation of a Mishnah-pericope, is not only *not* the product of logic (analogical-contrastive reasoning, hierarchical classification of the outcome), but is, and only can be, the product of exegesis of Scripture. That is only part of the matter, but that component of the larger judgment of Sifra's authorship does make the point that the Mishnah is subordinated to Scripture and validated only through Scripture. In that regard, the authorship of Sifra stands at one with the position of the authorships of the other successor-writings, even though Sifra's writers carried to a much more profound level of thought the critique of the Mishnah. They did so by rethinking the logical foundations of the entire Torah.

Sifra builds on two premises. First, it affirms the taxonomic logic of the Mishnah. Second, it insists that all taxonomy ultimately requires Scripture's guidance. Now we shall observe a sequence of cases in which Sifra's authorship demonstrates that Listenwissenschaft is a self-evidently valid mode of demonstrating the truth of propositions. Second, we shall note, in the same cases, that the source of the correct classification of things is Scripture and only Scripture. Without Scripture's intervention into the taxonomy of the world, we should have no knowledge at all of which things fall into which classifications and therefore are governed by which rules. Let us begin with a sustained example of the right way of doing things. Appropriately, the opening composition of Sifra shows is the contrast between relying on Scripture's classification, and the traits imputed by Scripture to the taxa it identifies, and appealing to categories not defined and endowed with indicative traits by Scripture.

Sifra I:I

1. A. "The Lord called [to Moses] and spoke [to him from the tent of meeting, saying, 'Speak to the Israelite people and say to them']" (Lev. 1:1):
   B. He gave priority to the calling over the speaking.
   C. That is in line with the usage of Scripture.
   D. Here there is an act of speaking, and in connection with the encounter at the bush [Ex. 3:4: "God called to him out of the bush, 'Moses, Moses'"], there is an act of speaking.
   E. Just as in the latter occasion, the act of calling is given priority over the act of speaking [even though the actual word, "speaking" does not occur, it is implicit in the framing of the verse], so here, with respect to the act of speaking, the act of calling is given priority over the act of speaking.
2. A. No [you cannot generalize on the basis of that case,] for if you invoke the case of the act of speaking at the bush, which is the first in the sequence of acts of speech [on which account, there had to be a call prior to entry into discourse],

Three. The Laws of Intellect: Sifra

- B. will you say the same of the act of speech in the tent of meeting, which assuredly is not the first in a sequence of acts of speech [so there was no need for a preliminary entry into discourse through a call]?
- C. The act of speech at Mount Sinai [Ex. 19:3] will prove to the contrary, for it is assuredly not the first in a sequence of acts of speech, yet, in that case, there was an act of calling prior to the act of speech.
- 3. A. No, [the exception proves nothing,] for if you invoke in evidence the act of speech at Mount Sinai, which pertained to all the Israelites, will you represent it as parallel to the act of speech in the tent of meeting, which is not pertinent to all Israel?
- B. Lo, you may sort matters out by appeal to comparison and contrast, specifically:
- C. The act of speech at the bush, which is the first of the acts of speech, is not of the same classification as the act of speech at Sinai, which is not the first act of speech.
- D. And the act of speech at Sinai, which is addressed to all Israel, is not in the same classification as the act of speech at the bush, which is not addressed to all Israel.
- 4. A. What they have in common, however, is that both of them are acts of speech, deriving from the mouth of the Holy One, addressed to Moses, in which case, the act of calling comes prior to the act of speech,
- B. so that, by way of generalization, we may maintain that every act of speech which comes from the mouth of the Holy One to Moses will be preceded by an act of calling.
- 5. A. Now if what the several occasions have in common is that all involve an act of speech, accompanied by fire, from the mouth of the Holy One, addressed to Moses, so that the act of calling was given priority over the act of speaking, then in every case in which there is an act of speech, involving fire, from the mouth of the Holy One, addressed to Moses, should involve an act of calling prior to the act of speech.
- B. But then an exception is presented by the act of speech at the tent of meeting, in which there was no fire.
- C. [That is why it was necessary for Scripture on this occasion to state explicitly,] "The Lord called [to Moses and spoke to him from the tent of meeting, saying, 'Speak to the Israelite people and say to them']" (Lev. 1:1).
- D. That explicit statement shows that, on the occasion at hand, priority was given to the act of calling over the act of speaking.
- I:II.1. A. ["The Lord called to Moses and spoke to him from the tent of meeting, saying, 'Speak to the Israelite people and say to them'" (Lev. 1:1)]: Might one suppose that the act of calling applied only to this act of speaking alone?

> B. And how on the basis of Scripture do we know that on the occasion of all acts of speaking that are mentioned in the Torah, [there was a prior act of calling]?
> C. Scripture specifies, "from the tent of meeting,"
> D. which bears the sense that on every occasion on which it was an act of speaking from the tent of meeting, there was an act of calling prior to the act of speaking.
> 2. A. Might one suppose that there was an act of calling only prior to the acts of speech alone?
> B. How on the basis of Scripture do I know that the same practice accompanied acts of saying and also acts of commanding?
> C. Said R. Simeon, "Scripture says not only, '...spoke,...,' but '...and he spoke,' [with the inclusion of the and] meant to encompass also acts of telling and also acts of commanding."

The exercise of generalization addresses the character of God's meeting with Moses. The point of special interest is the comparison of the meeting at the bush and the meeting at the tent of meeting. And at stake is asking whether all acts of God's calling and talking with, or speaking to, the prophet are the same, or whether some of these acts are of a different classification from others. In point of fact, we are able to come to a generalization, worked out at I:I.5.A. And that permits us to explain why there is a different usage at Lev. 1:1 from what characterizes parallel cases. I:II.1-2 proceeds to generalize from the case at hand to other usages entirely, a very satisfying conclusion to the whole. I separate I:II from I:I because had I:I ended at 5, it could have stood complete and on its own, and therefore I see I:II as a brief appendix. The interest for my argument should not be missed. We seek generalizations, governing rules, that are supposed to emerge by the comparison and contrast of categories or of classifications. The way to do this is to follow the usage of Scripture, that alone. And the right way of doing things is then illustrated.

How then do we appeal to Scripture to designate the operative classifications? Here is a simple example of the alternative mode of classification, one that does not appeal to the traits of things but to the utilization of names by Scripture. What we see is how by naming things in one way, rather than in another, Scripture orders all things, classifying and, in the nature of things, also hierarchizing them.

> **Sifra VII:V.**
> 1 A. "...and Aaron's sons the priests shall present the blood and throw the blood [round about against the altar that is at the door of the tent of meeting]:"
> B. Why does Scripture make use of the word "blood" twice [instead of using a pronoun]?
> C. [It is for the following purpose:] How on the basis of Scripture do you know that if blood deriving from one burnt offering was

Three. The Laws of Intellect: Sifra

confused with blood deriving from another burnt offering, blood deriving from one burnt offering with blood deriving from a beast that has been substituted therefor, blood deriving from a burnt offering with blood deriving from an unconsecrated beast, the mixture should nonetheless be presented?

D. It is because Scripture makes use of the word "blood" twice [instead of using a pronoun].

2. A. Is it possible to suppose that while if blood deriving from beasts in the specified classifications, it is to be presented, for the simple reason that if the several beasts while alive had been confused with one another, they might be offered up,

B. but how do we know that even if the blood of a burnt offering were confused with that of a beast killed as a guilt offering, [it is to be offered up}

C. I shall concede the case of the mixture of the blood of a burnt offering confused with that of a beast killed as a guilt offering, it is to be presented, for both this one and that one fall into the classification of Most Holy Things.

D. But how do I know that if the blood of a burnt offering were confused with the blood of a beast slaughtered in the classification of peace-offerings or of a thanksgiving offering, [it is to be presented]?

E. I shall concede the case of the mixture of the blood of a burnt offering confused with that of a beast slaughtered in the classification of peace-offerings or of a thanksgiving offering, [it is to be presented], because the beasts in both classifications produce blood that has to be sprinkled four times.

F. But how do I know that if the blood of a burnt offering were confused with the blood of a beast slaughtered in the classification of a firstling or a beast that was counted as tenth or of a beast designated as a Passover, [it is to be presented]?

G. I shall concede the case of the mixture of the blood of a burnt offering confused with that of a beast slaughtered in the classification of firstling or a beast that was counted as tenth or of a beast designated as a Passover, [it is to be presented], because Scripture uses the word "blood" two times.

H. Then while I may make that concession, might I also suppose that if the blood of a burnt offering was confused with the blood of beasts that had suffered an invalidation, it also may be offered up?

I. Scripture says, "...its blood," [thus excluding such a case].

J. Then I shall concede the case of a mixture of the blood of a valid burnt offering with the blood of beasts that had suffered an invalidation, which blood is not valid to be presented at all.

K. But how do I know that if such blood were mixed with the blood deriving from beasts set aside as sin-offerings to be offered on the inner altar, [it is not to be offered up]?

L. I can concede that the blood of a burnt offering that has been mixed with the blood deriving from beasts set aside as sin-offerings to be offered on the inner altar is not to be offered up, for the one is offered on the inner altar, and the other on the outer altar [the burnt offering brought as a free will offering, under discussion here, is slaughtered at the altar "...that is at the door of the tent of meeting," not at the inner altar].
M. But how do I know that even if the blood of a burnt offering was confused with the blood of sin-offerings that are to be slaughtered at the outer altar, it is not to be offered up?
N. Scripture says, "...its blood," [thus excluding such a case].

In place of rejecting arguments resting on classifying species into a common genus, we now demonstrate how classification really is to be carried on. It is through the imposition upon data of the categories dictated by Scripture: Scripture's use of language. That is the force of this powerful exercise. No. 1 sets the stage, simply pointing out that the use of the word "blood" twice encompasses a case in which blood in two distinct classifications is somehow confused in the process of the conduct of the cult. In such a case it is quite proper to pour out the mixture of blood deriving from distinct sources, e.g., beasts that have served different, but comparable purposes. We then systemically work out the limits of that rule, showing how comparability works, then pointing to cases in which comparability is set aside. Throughout the exposition, at the crucial point we invoke the formulation of Scripture, subordinating logic or in our instance the process of classification of like species to the dictation of Scripture. I cannot imagine a more successful demonstration of what the framers wish to say.

The authorship of Sifra never called into question the self-evident validity of taxonomic logic. Its critique is addressed only to how the Mishnah's framers identify the origins of, and delineate, taxa. But that critique proves fundamental to the case that that authorship proposed to make. For, intending to demonstrate that the Torah was a proper noun, and that everything that was valid came to expression in the single, cogent statement of the Torah, the authorship at hand identified the fundamental issue. It is the debate over the way we know things. In insisting, in agreement with the framers of the Mishnah, that there are not only cases but also rules, not only species but also genera, the authorship of Sifra also made its case in behalf of the case for the Torah as a proper noun. This carries us to the theological foundation for Sifra's authorship's sustained critique of applied reason.

II. To whom, and for whom, does the document speak?
Propositions and preoccupations

The Mishnah's framers' principle of speciation had appealed to the intrinsic traits, the nature, of things. The contrary claim, implicit throughout Sifra's critique of the Mishnah, said that, without the revelation of the Torah, the human intellect can identify in the end only species, no genera. Sifra's authorship also maintained that many things never can become one thing except God makes them so and tells us in the Torah. To these allegations the Mishnah's composers would respond by adducing the evidence at hand: things speak for themselves. They would (in this hypothetical argument) demonstrate that the created world exhibits not chaos but order and a regularity we can ourselves uncover. The critique of this position can be shown to contradict the facts of the palpable world, the creation of which, after all, the Torah describes.

The document speaks, then, for those preoccupied with the primacy, over analytical reason, of Scripture, a.k.a., the written Torah, in the Torah of Sinai. Time and again Sifra's authorship demonstrates that the formation of classifications based on monothetic taxonomy, that is to say, traits that are not only common to both items but that are shared throughout both of the items subject to comparison and contrast, simply will not serve. For at every point at which someone alleges uniform, that is to say, monothetic likeness, Sifra's authorship will demonstrate difference. Then how to proceed? Will it be appeal to some shared traits as a basis for classification: this is not like that, and that is not like this, but the indicative trait that both exhibit is such and so, that is to say, polythetic taxonomy? No, that is not a reliable solution. For the self-evident problem in accepting differences among things and insisting, nonetheless, on their monomorphic character for purposes of comparison and contrast, cannot be set aside: *who says*? That is, if I can adduce in evidence for a shared classification of things only a few traits among many characteristic of each thing, then what stops me from treating all things alike? Polythetic taxonomy opens the way to an unlimited exercise in finding what diverse things have in common and imposing, for that reason, one rule on everything. Then the very working of *Listenwissenschaft* as a tool of analysis, differentiation, comparison, contrast, and the descriptive determination of rules yields the opposite of what is desired.

III. Implicit Truths

The upshot is very simple. The authorship of Sifra concurs in the fundamental principle that right thinking requires discovering the classification of things and determining the rule that governs diverse things. That authorship differs from the view of the Mishnah's concerns — I again emphasize — about *the origins of taxa*. Precisely how do we know what diverse things form a single classification of things? The answer of this discourse in the form of a commentary is, taxa originate in Scripture. They are not discovered by inherent traits but are revealed from above. Accordingly, at stake in the critique of the Mishnah are the principles of logic necessary for understanding the construction and inner structure of creation.

In appealing to the principle, for taxonomy, of *sola Scriptura*, I mean to set forth what I conceive really to be at stake. It is the character of the Torah and what it is, in the Torah, the thing that we wish to discern. In their delineation of correct hierarchical logic, Sifra's authors uncovered, within the Torah an adumbration of the working of the mind of God. That is because the premise of all discourse is that the Torah was written by God and dictated by God to Moses at Sinai. And that will in the end explain why our authorship for its part has entered into the Torah long passages of not merely clarification but active intrusion, making itself a component of the interlocutorial process.

We have concentrated upon Sifra's authorship's mordant critique of applied reason. Its rehabilitation of the available system of reason was accomplished in such a way as to reopen the entire question of the definition of the Torah. By returning to Scripture as the source for taxa, by appealing to Scripture, and Scripture alone, as the criterion for like and unlike, and by then restating the whole of Scripture, for the book of Leviticus, to encompass words not in the original, written Torah but only in the other, oral Torah, the Mishnah for example, that authorship exhibited remarkable imagination.

The authorship of Sifra proposed to regain access to the modes of thought that guided the formation of the Torah, oral and written alike: comparison and contrast in this way, not in that, identification of categories in one manner, not in another. Since those were the modes of thought that, in our authorship's conception, dictated the structure of intellect upon which the Torah, the united Torah, rested, a simple conclusion is the sole possible one. Now to answer the question of the basis on which our authorship represented itself as participants in, and interlocutors of, the Torah, such that they were prepared to re-present, that is to say, simply rewrite the Torah.

In their analysis of the deepest structures of intellect of the Torah, the authorship of Sifra supposed to enter into the mind of God, showing how God's mind worked when God formed the Torah, written and oral alike. And there, in the intellect of God, in their judgment humanity gained access to the only means of uniting the Torah, because that is where the Torah originated. But in discerning how God's mind worked, the intellectuals who created Sifra claimed for themselves a place in that very process of thought that had given birth to the Torah. Our authorship could rewrite the Torah because, knowing how the Torah originally was written, they too could write (though not reveal) the Torah.

No wonder an Israelite who says the Torah does not come from Heaven loses his portion in the world to come.

4

The Laws of History: Genesis Rabbah

I. THE DOCUMENT AND ITS PROGRAM: RECURRENT QUESTIONS

Sifra's framers took as their problem the character of the Torah and produced a theoretical demonstration of the meaning of monotheism in the framework of natural history. Their analysis repeatedly demonstrated in the manner of the Mishnah that many things derive from one thing, one thing absorbs many things. But these abstractions of natural history ignored the diversity of human experience over time and in society, the complexity of particular events and persons, the disorder of what we call history. Monotheism set forth as an ontological principle of nature and the social order therefore proved necessary but insufficient. The dynamism of human affairs contradicted claims in behalf of the unity of being. Monotheism demonstrated out of the materials of history would match the achievement of the intellects of Sifra.

The Rabbinic sages had therefore to answer the question, In what way do the dynamic character of the social order and its singular happenings attest to the unity, if not the uniformity, of human events? We should call the question historical, and so would the biblical narrators who produced the canon from Genesis through Kings: an unfolding story with a beginning, middle, and end. But what we mean by history and how the Rabbinic sages sorted out the unit of human events do not match. For one thing, history requires the division between past, present, and future, the intrusion of memory and the conviction of the presence of the past as much as the pastness of the present, none of which characterized the Rabbinic conception. Stated in so many words: "considerations of 'before' and 'after' do not apply to the Torah," which portrays eternity in time.

Accordingly, the issue of how the social order — using conventional terms: the events of history, the patterns of the past — bears out the implicit messages of monotheism concerning the unity of all being under the governance of one God —

that issue dominated. It formed the logical next step beyond the dominant question of Sifra, ca. 300. Genesis Rabbah, a commentary on the book of Genesis that reached closure about a century after Sifra, in ca. 400 C.E., addressed that question. The answer presented itself in the claim that rational rules governed history as much as nature, patterns prevailed, the future matched the past in conforming to paradigms, and laws of history, no less than laws of nature, inhere in the Torah. The Torah is explicit, for example at Leviticus 26, that actions of a given type precipitate results of a determinate sort, and that generalization finds particularization through a discerning examination of Scripture. It is then possible also to predict the future. One need only know the rules that prevail, the pattern of the past that is perpetually present.

The unity of human events comes to the surface in the treatment of Genesis's stories of the patriarchs and matriarchs as the paradigm for the history of their descendants, the children of Israel, through time. It pervades the disposition of the comparison of Abraham's biography and future Israel's history. It dominates in the presentation of the histories of Israel and the four monarchies, Babylonia, Media, Greece, Rome, as a single paradigm and as governed by a single law of justice. Israel and the four monarchies are subject to the same law, and Israelite tribes form counterparts to the four monarchies:

Genesis Rabbah XCIX:II.
1. A. "For the Lord God will do nothing unless he reveals his secret to his servants the prophets" (Amos 3:7).
   B. Jacob linked two of his sons, corresponding to two of the monarchies, and Moses linked two of the tribes, corresponding to two of the monarchies.
   C. Judah corresponds to the kingdom of Babylonia, for this is compared to a lion and that is compared to a lion. This is compared to a lion: "Judah is a lion's whelp" (Gen. 49:9), and so too Babylonia: "The first was like a lion" (Dan. 7:4).
   D. Then by the hand of which of the tribes will the kingdom of Babylonia fall? It will be by the hand of Daniel, who comes from the tribe of Judah.
   E. Benjamin corresponds to the kingdom of Media, for this is compared to a wolf and that is compared to a wolf. This is compared to a wolf: "Benjamin is a ravenous wolf, [in the morning devouring the prey, and at even dividing the spoil]." And that is compared to a wolf: "And behold, another beast, a second, like a wolf" (Dan. 7:5).
   H. Then by the hand of which of the tribes will the kingdom of Media fall? It will be by the hand of Mordecai, who comes from the tribe of Benjamin.
   I. Levi corresponds to the kingdom of Greece. This is the third tribe in order, and that is the third kingdom in order. This is written with a word that is made up of three letters, and that is written with a

Four. The Laws of History: Genesis Rabbah

word which consists of three letters. This one sounds the horn and that one sounds the horn, this one wears turbans and that one wears helmets, this one wears pants and that one wears knee-cuts.

J. To be sure, this one is very populous, while that one is few in numbers. But the many came and fell into the hand of the few.

K. On account of merit deriving from what source did this take place? It is on account of the blessing that Moses bestowed: "Smite through the loins of them that rise up against him" (Deut. 33:11).

L. Then by the hand of which of the tribes will the kingdom of Greece fall? It will be by the hand of sons of the Hasmoneans, who come from the tribe of Levi.'

M. Joseph corresponds to the kingdom of Edom [Rome], for this one has horns and that one has horns. This one has horns: "His firstling bullock, majesty is his, and his horns are the horns of the wild ox" (Deut. 33:17). And that one has horns: "And concerning the ten horns that were on its head" (Dan. 7:20). This one kept away from fornication while that one cleaved to fornication. This one paid respect for the honor owing to his father, while that one despised the honor owing to his father. Concerning this one it is written, "For I fear God" (Gen. 42:18), while in regard to that one it is written, "And he did not fear God" (Deut. 25:18). [So the correspondence in part is one of opposites.]

N. Then by the hand of which of the tribes will the kingdom of Edom fall? It will be by the hand of the anointed for war, who comes from the tribe of Joseph.

O. R. Phineas in the name of R. Samuel b. Nahman: "There is a tradition that Esau will fall only by the hand of the sons of Rachel: 'Surely the least of the flock shall drag them away' (Jer. 49:20). Why the least? Because they are the youngest of the tribes."

Judah matches the first kingdom, Babylonia, which will fall to Daniel, member of Judah's tribe, Benjamin matches Media, which will fall to Mordecai, Levi corresponds with Greece, which will fall to the Hasmoneans, of the tribe of Levi, and Joseph corresponds with Rome, which will fall to the Messiah assigned to war. What is important to our problem is the premise: a single pattern governs Israel and the world-empires, and, in Israel, the family of the patriarchs.

We survey just a few of the demonstrations in Genesis Rabbah that a rational paradigm governs human events. The first task is to show whence comes knowledge of the paradigm, and the answer of Genesis Rabbah conforms to that of Sifra: the Torah properly paradigmatized reveals the future history of Israel and the nations, because it matches the governing principles of nature and history alike. That abstract claim takes on specificity: the Torah shows that the future history of Israel and the nations was present from the very creation of the world. The dynamism of human affairs conforms to the simple laws that regulate creation as well:

Genesis Rabbah II:III.

1. A. ["And the earth was unformed..." (Gen. 1:2):]
   B. R. Judah b. R. Simon interpreted the verse as referring to coming generations, [as follows]:
   C. "'The earth was unformed' refers to Adam, who was reduced to complete nothingness [on account of his sin].
   D. "'And void' refers to Cain, who sought to return the world to unformedness and void.
   E. "'And darkness was upon the face of the deep' (Gen. 1:2) refers to the generation of Enosh: 'And their works are in the dark' (Is. 29:15).
   F. "'Upon the face of the deep' (Gen. 1:2) refers to the generation of the flood: 'On the same day were all the fountains of the great deep broken up' (Gen. 7:11).
   G. "'And the spirit of God hovered over the face of the water' (Gen. 1:2): 'And God made a wind pass over the earth' (Gen. 8:1).
   H. "Said the Holy One, blessed be he, 'For how long will the world make its way in darkness. Let light come.'
   I. "'And God said, "Let there be light"' (Gen. 1:3). This refers to Abraham. That is in line with the following verse of Scripture: 'Who has raised up one from the earth, whom he calls in righteousness to his foot' (Is. 41:23).
   J. "'And God called the light day' (Gen. 1:3) refers to Jacob.
   K. "'And the darkness he called night' (Gen. 1:30) refers to Esau.
   L. "'And there was evening' refers to Esau.
   M. "'And there was morning' refers to Jacob.
   N. "'One day'— for the Holy One, blessed be he, gave him one day, and what is that day? It is the Day of Atonement. [Freedman, p. 17, n. 1: It is the one day over which Satan, symbolizing the wickedness of Esau, has no power.]"

Genesis Rabbah II:IV.

1. A. R. Simeon b. Laqish interpreted the verses at hand to speak of the empires [of the historical age to come].
   B. "'The earth was unformed' refers to Babylonia, 'I beheld the earth and lo, it was unformed' (Jer. 4:23).
   C. "'And void' refers to Media: 'They hasted [using the letters of the same root as the word for void] to bring Haman' (Est. 6:14).
   D. "'Darkness' refers to Greece, which clouded the vision of the Israelites through its decrees, for it said to Israel, 'Write on the horn of an ox [as a public proclamation for all to see] that you have no portion in the God of Israel.'
   E. "'...upon the face of the deep' refers to the wicked kingdom [of Rome].
   F. "Just as the deep surpasses investigation, so the wicked kingdom surpasses investigation.

Four. The Laws of History: Genesis Rabbah

G. "'And the spirit of God hovers' refers to the spirit of the Messiah, in line with the following verse of Scripture: 'And the spirit of the Lord shall rest upon him' (Is. 11:2)."

Each step in the creation-story finds its counterpart in the narrative of humanity, from Adam to Abraham. Adam, Cain, the generation of Enosh, of the flood, are matched by Abraham, Jacob-Esau, and the Day of Atonement. What is important for us is the correspondence between the formlessness of the earth and Adam, the void and Cain, the darkness and Enosh, the generation of the flood, giving way to Abraham, source of light. Then, J-M, comes the contrast between Jacob and Esau, light and darkness, finally coming to the climax of the Day of Atonement. J-N look like a separate composition, but the whole serves to illustrate the main point, which is the correspondence of nature and history. II:IV.1 moves on to the familiar motif, the world-empires, Babylonia, Media, Greece, and Rome, with Israel forming the fifth and final monarchy with the advent of the Messiah. Here we have two exercises that express the same conviction, which is that nature and the narrative of human history correspond. A single pattern emerges from both, darkness representing wickedness, light, goodness, and so throughout. What is right on the surface is that the Torah properly read contains the key to the story of humanity.

A still more explicit statement that creation matches the history of humanity identifies the rivers flowing out of Eden with the world-empires, so nature matches the dynamic of human events we know as history:

Genesis Rabbah XVI:IV.

1. A. R. Tanhuma in the name of R. Joshua b. Levi said to him, "In the future the Holy One, blessed be he, is destined to give a cup of bitterness to the nations to drink from the place from which this [river] goes forth. And what is the verse that so indicates? 'A river flowed out of Eden to water the garden' (Gen. 2:10).
   B. "This refers to the four kingdoms, forming the counterpart to the four heads [into which the river is divided].
   C. "The name of the first is Pishon' (Gen. 2:11) refers to Babylonia, in line with this verse: 'And their horsemen spread (*pashu*) themselves' (Hab. 1:8). And it also responds to the midget dwarf, who was smaller than a handbreadth [that is, Nebuchadnezzar].
   D. "'It is the one which flows around the whole land of Havilah' [again, referring to Babylonia,] for [Nebuchadnezzar] came up and encompassed the entire Land of Israel, concerning which it is written, 'Hope you in God, for I shall yet praise him' (Ps. 42:6). [There is a play on the words for Havilah and hope.]
   H. "'And the name of the second river is Gihon' refers to Media, for Haman [who was a Median] had [because of his deranged hatred of Israel] inflamed eyes like those of a serpent, on the count: 'On your belly (GHWNK) you will go, and dust you will eat all the days of your life' (Gen. 3:14).

I. "It is the one which flows around the whole land of Cush' (Gen. 2:13). This allusion is to [Ahasueros, the Median, as in this verse]: 'Who reigned from India even to Cush' (Est. 1:1).

J. "'And the name of the third river is Tigris' (Gen. 2:14) refers to Greece, which was sharp and speedy in making evil decrees, saying to Israel, 'Write on the horn of an ox [as a public proclamation] that you have no share in the God of Israel.'"

4. A. "And the fourth river is the Euphrates" (Gen. 2:14):
   B. This refers to Rome.
   C. It is called the Euphrates (PRT) because it unsettled and harassed his world.
   D. It is called the Euphrates because it became abundant on account of the blessing of the old man [Jacob, who blessed Esau, standing for Rome].
   E. It is called the Euphrates because: "In the future I am going to destroy it, at the end."
   F. It is called the Euphrates because of what will happen at the end of it: "I have trodden the winepress alone" (Is. 63:3).

The first river corresponds with Babylonia for the reasons given, the second refers to Media, the third to Greece, and the fourth to Rome. Once more, history and nature correspond, with nature embodying the chief players of history. But that affirmation of a simple principle paramount in human events — the match of nature and the social order of nations — raises more questions than it settles. For at stake throughout is what happens to Israel, and the data that require explanation derive from Israel's existence over time.

The details subject to rationalization derive from the narratives of Genesis that pertain to the patriarchs and matriarchs. These narratives prefigure the later history of Israel. So the key to the rationality of the governing principles of human events lies in the actions of the founding generations of Israel. That establishes the unifying paradigm joining the generations and establishing a single rule that governs them all.

Genesis Rabbah XL:VI.

1. A. "And for her sake he dealt well with Abram" (Gen. 12:16):
   B. "And Pharaoh gave men orders concerning him, [and they set him on the way, with his wife and all that he had]" (Gen. 12:20).
   C. R. Phineas in the name of R. Hoshaiah said, "The Holy One, blessed be he, said to our father, Abraham, 'Go and pave a way before your children.' [Set an example for them, so that whatever you do now, they will do later on.] [We shall now see how each statement about Abram at Gen. 12:10-20 finds a counterpart in the later history of Israel, whether Jacob or the children of Jacob.]
   D. "You find that whatever is written in regard to our father, Abraham, is written also with regard to his children.

Four. The Laws of History: Genesis Rabbah

E. "With regard to Abraham it is written, 'And there was a famine in the land' (Gen. 12:10) In connection with Israel: 'For these two years has the famine been in the land" (Gen. 45:6).

F. "With regard to Abraham: 'And Abram went down into Egypt' (Gen. 12:10).

G. "With regard to Israel: 'And our fathers went down into Egypt' (Num. 20:15).

H. "With regard to Abraham: 'To sojourn there' (Gen. 12:10).

I. "With regard to Israel: 'To sojourn in the land we have come' (Gen. 47:4).

J. "With regard to Abraham: 'For the famine is heavy in the land' (Gen. 12:10).

K. "With regard to Israel: 'And the famine was heavy in the land' (Gen. 43:1).

L. "With regard to Abraham: 'And it came to pass, when he drew near to enter into Egypt' (Gen. 12:11: 'When he was about to enter Egypt').

M. "With regard to Israel: 'And when Pharaoh drew near' (Ex. 14:10).

N. "With regard to Abraham: 'And they will kill me but you will they keep alive' (Gen. 12:12).

O. "With regard to Israel: 'Every son that is born you shall cast into the river, and every daughter you shall save alive' (Ex. 1:22).

P. "With regard to Abraham: 'Say you are my sister, that it may go well with me because of you' (Gen. 12:13).

Q. "With regard to Israel: 'And God dealt well with the midwives' (Ex. 1:20).

R. "With regard to Abraham: 'And when Abram had entered Egypt' (Gen. 12:14).

S. "Israel: 'Now these are the names of the sons of Israel, who came into Egypt' (Ex. 1:1).

T. "With regard to Abraham: 'And Abram was very rich in cattle, in silver, and in gold' (Gen. 13:23).

U. "With regard to Israel: 'And he brought them forth with silver and gold' (Ps. 105:37).

V. "With regard to Abraham: 'And Pharaoh gave men orders concerning him and they set him on the way' (Gen. 12:20).

W. "With regard to Israel: 'And the Egyptians were urgent upon the people to send them out' (Ex. 12:33).

X. "With regard to Abraham: 'And he went on his journeys' (Gen. 13:3).

Y. "With regard to Israel: 'These are the journeys of the children of Israel' (Num. 33:1)."

The Israelites did what Abraham did. He went down to Egypt, so did they; it was to sojourn through the famine, and so throughout. The details here are less important than what is implicit: the uniform actions of the patriarch and of his descendants. So a pattern is established. A more weighty claim follows:

Genesis Rabbah XLII:II.
2. A. Said R. Abin, "Just as [Israel's history] began with the encounter with four kingdoms, so [Israel's history] will conclude with the encounter with the four kingdoms.
   B. "'Chedorlaomer, king of Elam, Tidal, king of Goiim, Amraphel, king of Shinar, and Arioch, king of Ellasar, four kings against five' (Gen. 14:9).
   C. "So [Israel's history] will conclude with the encounter with the four kingdoms: the kingdom of Babylonia, the kingdom of Medea, the kingdom of Greece, and the kingdom of Edom."

Here is a fine example of identifying a paradigm, with the outcome of predicting the future. The pattern is simple: when we know the initial pattern, we know the shape of the concluding pattern. Israel's history began with the encounter with the four kingdoms, so it will conclude with the encounter with the four kingdoms.

To establish a pattern more than a single iteration is required. Accordingly, we ask whether there are other cases in the corpus of facts provided by Scripture that yield the same pattern. Here we see how that paradigm is embodied in the "covenant between the pieces" of Genesis 15, where the entirety of Israelite history is embodied in the offering:

Genesis Rabbah XLIV:XV.
1. A. Another matter: "Bring me a heifer three years old, [a she-goat three years old, a ram three years old, a turtledove, and a young pigeon]" (Gen. 15:9):
   B. "Bring me a heifer three years old" refers to Babylonia, that produced three [kings important in Israel's history], Nebuchadnezzar, Evil Merodach, and Balshazzar.
   C. "...a she-goat three years old" refers to Media, that also produced three kings, Cyrus, Darius, and Ahasuerus.
   D. "...a ram three years old" refers to Greece.
   I. "...a turtledove, and a young pigeon" (Gen. 15:9) refers to Edom. It was a turtle-dove that would rob.

Genesis Rabbah XLIV:XVI.
1. A. "And when birds of prey came down upon the carcasses, Abram drove them away" (Gen. 15:11):
   B. Said R. Assi, "Abraham took a staff and beat them, but they were not beaten. Nonetheless: 'Abram drove them away' by means of repentance." [Freedman, p. 372, n. 1: The birds of prey represent the nations swooping down on Israel. Abram tried to beat them off by physical force but without success, and it is only when Israel turns to God in penitence that his enemies are driven off.]

Genesis Rabbah XLIV:XVII.

4. A. "[And it came to pass, as the sun was going down,] lo, a deep sleep fell on Abram, and lo, a dread and great darkness fell upon him" (Gen. 15:12):

B. "...lo, a dread" refers to Babylonia, as it is written, "Then was Nebuchadnezzar filled with fury" (Gen. 3:19).

C. "...and darkness" refers to Media, which darkened the eyes of Israel by making it necessary for the Israelites to fast and conduct public mourning.

D. "...great..." refers to Greece.

G. "...fell upon him" refers to Edom, as it is written, "The earth quakes at the noise of their fall" (Jer. 49:21).

H. Some reverse matters:

I. "...fell upon him" refers to Babylonia, since it is written, "Fallen, fallen is Babylonia" (Is. 21:9).

J. "...great..." refers to Media, in line with this verse: "King Ahasuerus did make great" (Est. 3:1).

K. "...and darkness" refers to Greece, which darkened the eyes of Israel by its harsh decrees.

L. "...lo, a dread" refers to Edom, as it is written, "After this I saw...,a fourth beast, dreadful and terrible" (Dan. 7:7).

Genesis Rabbah XLIV:XVIII.

1. A. "Then the Lord said to Abram, 'Know of a surety [that your descendants will be sojourners in a land that is not theirs, and they will be slaves there, and they will be oppressed for four hundred years; but I will bring judgment on the nation which they serve, and afterward they shall come out with great possessions']" (Gen. 15:13-14):

B. "Know" that I shall scatter them.

C. "Of a certainty" that I shall bring them back together again.

D. "Know" that I shall put them out as a pledge [in expiation of their sins].

E. "Of a certainty" that I shall redeem them.

F. "Know" that I shall make them slaves.

G. "Of a certainty" that I shall free them.

2. A. "...that your descendants will be sojourners in a land that is not theirs and they will be slaves there, and they will be oppressed for four hundred years:"

B. It is four hundred years from the point at which you will produce a descendant. [The Israelites will not serve as slaves for four hundred years, but that figure refers to the passage of time from Isaac's birth.]

C. Said R. Yudan, "The condition of being outsiders, the servitude, the oppression in a land that was not theirs all together would last for four hundred years, that was the requisite term."

Genesis Rabbah XLIV:XIX.

1. A. "But I will also bring judgment on the nation which they serve" (Gen. 15:14):

   B. Said R. Helbo, "Rather than, 'and that nation,' the passage states, 'But I will *also* bring judgment on the nation which they serve' (Gen. 15:14). Also they, also Egypt and the four kingdoms who will enslave you [will God judge]."

Genesis Rabbah XLIV:XXI.

2. A. "...behold a smoking fire pot and a flaming torch passed between these pieces" (Gen. 15:17):

   B. Simeon bar Abba in the name of R. Yohanan: "He showed him four things, Gehenna, the [four] kingdoms, the giving of the Torah, and the sanctuary. He said to him, 'So long as your descendants are occupied with these latter two, they will be saved from the former two. If they abandon two of them, they will be judged by the other two.'

   C. "He said to him, 'What is your preference? Do you want your children to go down into Gehenna or to be subjugated to the four kingdoms?'"

   D. R. Hinena bar Pappa said, "Abraham chose for himself the subjugation to the four kingdoms."

   E. R. Yudan and R. Idi and R. Hama bar Hanina: "Abraham chose for himself Gehenna, but the Holy One, blessed be he, chose the subjugation to the four kingdoms for him."

3. A. R. Huna in the name of R. Aha: "Now Abraham sat and puzzled all that day, saying, 'Which should I choose?'

   B. "Said the Holy One, blessed be he, to him, 'Choose without delay.' That is in line with this verse: 'On that day the Lord made a covenant with Abram' (Gen. 15:18)."

   C. This brings us to the dispute of R. Hinena bar Pappa with R. Yudan and R. Idi and R. Hama bar Haninah.

   D. R. Hinena bar Pappa said, "Abraham chose for himself the subjugation to the four kingdoms."

   E. R. Yudan and R. Idi and R. Hama bar Haninah said in the name of a single sage in the name of Rabbi: "The Holy One, blessed be he, chose the subjugation to the four kingdoms for him, in line with the following verse of Scripture: 'You have caused men to ride over our heads' (Ps. 66:12). That is to say, you have made ride over our heads various nations, and it is as though 'we went through fire and through water' (Ps. 66:21)."

   F. R. Joshua said, "Also the splitting of the Red Sea he showed him, as it is written, 'That passed between these pieces' (Gen. 15:17), along the lines of the verse, 'O give thanks to him who divided the Red Sea in two' [in which the same word, the letters for pieces, occurs as 'in two'] (Ps. 86:13)."

Four. The Laws of History: Genesis Rabbah

This elaborate demonstration shows us the presence of a system and a plan that animate all of human events. XLIV:XV.1 has Jacob contemplate the four monarchies, Babylonia, Media, Greece, and Rome, in the specified offerings. Abraham overcame the bids of prey, the nations, by repentance. He saw the nations in his dream, XLIV:XVII.4. XLIV:XVIII.1 has Abraham review the future history of Israel, exile and restoration, enslaved and redeemed. No. 2 goes over the same ground. XLIV:XXI.2 has Abraham select Israel's future: subjugation to the four kingdoms rather than going down into Gehenna.

But a system must be systematic, and how the regularities play themselves out demands attention. The components of the pattern require definition. They encompass three phases, matching past, present, and future: Israel in the wilderness, Israel in the Land, and Israel in the world to come. The following composition shows how Abraham's transaction with the three angels before the fall of Sodom, Gen. 18:1ff., yielded a result for Israel in the wilderness and Israel in the Land of Israel and Israel in the age to come.

Genesis Rabbah XLVIII:X.

1. A. He lifted up his eyes and looked, and behold, three men stood in front of him. When he saw them, he ran from the tent door to meet them and bowed himself to the earth and said, 'My lord, if I have found favor in your sight, do not pass by your servant'" (Gen. 18:3):
2. A. "Let a little water be brought" (Gen. 18:4):
   B. Said to him the Holy One, blessed be he, "You have said, 'Let a little water be brought' (Gen. 18:4). By your life, I shall pay your descendants back for this: 'Then sang Israel this song," spring up O well, sing you to it'" (Num. 21:7)."
   C. That recompense took place in the wilderness. Where do we find that it took place in the Land of Israel as well?
   D. "A land of brooks of water" (Deut. 8:7).
   E. And where do we find that it will take place in the age to come?
   F. "'"And it shall come to pass in that day that living waters shall go out of Jerusalem" (Zech. 14:8).
   G. ["And wash your feet" (Gen. 18:4)]: [Said to him the Holy One, blessed be he,] "You have said, 'And wash your feet.' By your life, I shall pay your descendants back for this: 'Then I washed you in water' (Ez. 16:9)."
   H. That recompense took place in the wilderness. Where do we find that it took place in the Land of Israel as well?
   I. "Wash you, make you clean" (Is. 1:16).
   J. And where do we find that it will take place in the age to come?
   K. "When the Lord will have washed away the filth of the daughters of Zion" (Is. 4:4).
   L. [Said to him the Holy One, blessed be he,] "You have said, 'And rest yourselves under the tree' (Gen. 18:4). By your life, I shall

pay your descendants back for this: 'He spread a cloud for a screen' (Ps. 105:39)."
M. That recompense took place in the wilderness. Where do we find that it took place in the Land of Israel as well?
N. "You shall dwell in booths for seven days" (Lev. 23:42).
O. And where do we find that it will take place in the age to come?
P. "And there shall be a pavilion for a shadow in the day-time from the heat" (Is. 4:6).
Q. [Said to him the Holy One, blessed be he,] "You have said, 'While I fetch a morsel of bread that you may refresh yourself' (Gen. 18:5). By your life, I shall pay your descendants back for this: 'Behold I will cause to rain bread from heaven for you' (Ex. 16:45)"
R. That recompense took place in the wilderness. Where do we find that it took place in the Land of Israel as well?
S. "A land of wheat and barley" (Deut. 8:8).
T. And where do we find that it will take place in the age to come?
U. "He will be as a rich grain field in the land" (Ps. 82:16).
V. [Said to him the Holy One, blessed be he,] "You ran after the herd ['And Abraham ran to the herd' (Gen. 18:7)]. By your life, I shall pay your descendants back for this: 'And there went forth a wind from the Lord and brought across quails from the sea' (Num. 11:27)."
W. That recompense took place in the wilderness. Where do we find that it took place in the Land of Israel as well?
X. "Now the children of Reuben and the children of Gad had a very great multitude of cattle" (Num. 32:1).
Y. And where do we find that it will take place in the age to come?
Z. ""And it will come to pass in that day that a man shall rear a young cow and two sheep" (Is. 7:21).
AA. [Said to him the Holy One, blessed be he,] "You stood by them: 'And he stood by them under the tree while they ate' (Gen. 18:8). By your life, I shall pay your descendants back for this: 'And the Lord went before them' (Ex. 13:21)."
BB. That recompense took place in the wilderness. Where do we find that it took place in the Land of Israel as well?
CC. "God stands in the congregation of God" (Ps. 82:1).
DD. And where do we find that it will take place in the age to come?
EE. "The breaker is gone up before them...and the Lord at the head of them" (Mic. 2:13).

The three components of Israel's future history form the framework for this construction. Each gesture of Abraham found its match in all three ages, bringing water, washing feet, rest in the shade, bringing bread, providing meat, standing over and serving the angels. Israel's traverse of the wilderness, its possession of the Land, and its entry into the world to come, all respond to details of Abraham's conduct. A single pattern governs through the coming ages.

Israel's future history is captured in mute symbolism, not only narrative:

Genesis Rabbah LXXXVIII:V.
1. A. ["So the chief butler told his dream to Joseph and said to him, 'In my dream there was a vine before me, and on the vine there were three branches; as soon as it budded, its blossoms shot forth, and the clusters ripened into grapes. Pharaoh's cup was in my hand, and I took the grapes and pressed them into Pharaoh's cup and placed the cup in Pharaoh's hand. And I took the grapes and pressed them into Pharaoh's cup and placed the cup in Pharaoh's hand'" (Gen. 49:11-13)]. "...there was a vine before me:" this refers to Israel: "You plucked up a vine out of Egypt" (Ps. 80:9).
2. A. "'Pharaoh's cup was in my hand, and I took the grapes and pressed them into Pharaoh's cup and placed the cup in Pharaoh's hand. And I took the grapes and pressed them into Pharaoh's cup and placed the cup in Pharaoh's hand.'...' you shall place Pharaoh's cup in his hand:'"
   B. On what basis did sages ordain that there should be four cups of wine for Passover?
   C. R. Hunah in the name of R. Benaiah: "They correspond to the four times that redemption is stated with respect to Egypt: 'I will bring you out...and I will deliver you...and I will redeem you...and I will take you' (Ex. 6:6-7)."
   D. R. Samuel b. Nahman said, "They correspond to the four times that 'cups' are mentioned here: 'Pharaoh's *cup* was in my hand, and I took the grapes and pressed them into Pharaoh's *cup* and placed the *cup* in Pharaoh's hand. And I took the grapes and pressed them into Pharaoh's *cup*.'"
   E. R. Levi said, "They correspond to the four kingdoms."
   F. R. Joshua b. Levi said, "They correspond to the four cups of fury that the Holy One, blessed be he, will give the nations of the world to drink: 'For thus says the Lord, the God of Israel, to me, "Take this cup of the wine of fury"' (Jer. 25:15). 'Babylon has been a golden cup in the Lord's hand' (Jer. 51:7). 'For in the hand of the Lord there is a cup' (Ps. 75:9). 'And burning wind shall be the portion of their cup' (Ps. 11:6).
   G. "And in response to these, the Holy One, blessed be he, will give Israel four cups of salvation to drink in the age to come: 'O Lord, the portion of my inheritance and of my cup, you maintain my lot' (Ps. 16:5). 'You prepare a table before me in the presence of my enemies, you have anointed my head with oil, my cup runs over' (Ps. 23:5). 'I will lift up the cup of salvations and call upon the name of the Lord' (Ps. 116:13).
   H. "What is said is not 'cup of salvation' but 'cup of salvations,' one in the days of the Messiah, the other in the time of Gog and Magog."

The four references to "cup" correspond to the four kingdoms, the four cups of fury that God will give the nations of the world to drink, the four cups of salvation that Israel will drink.

In these and other ways the cogency of human events matches the unity of nature in a massive recapitulation of monotheism through creation and nature, human events and the outcome of those events in time and eternity. Ontological monotheism finds its match in the outcome of the exegesis of the Scriptural narrative. How is this the case? The story of humanity yields what we may call paradigmatic monotheism, the governance of a few uniform and mutually cogent patterns over the complexities of human history and destiny. A few simple rules emerge. The specificities of the pattern are few, the illustrations dense and complex, just as the Mishnah sets forth through an unlimited range and number of demonstrations in concrete data a few simple propositions concerning the one and the many.

II. To whom, and for whom, does the document speak? Propositions and preoccupations

The preoccupation with the patterns that form a single framework out of past, present, and future expresses the monotheist conviction of the unity of human existence. The complexities of time and change when properly sorted out yield the simplicity of monotheism: a few coherent patterns govern throughout. The document speaks for those that transcend the historical lessons of events, such as are portrayed in Scripture's narrative from Genesis through Kings. Now a new mode of thought presents an implicit, and devastating critique of historical thinking in behalf of paradigmatic analysis.

No boundary distinguished past from present; time was understood in a completely different way. Within the conception of time that formed consciousness and culture, the past formed a perpetual presence, the present took place on the plane of the past, and no lines of structure or order distinguished the one from the other. Events thus are to be classified and regularized, treated as data of natural history as much as the indicative qualities of an oven or of an antelope are. A historical way of thinking about past, present, and future, time and eternity, the here and now in relationship to the ages, — that is, Scripture's way of thinking — gave way to another mode of thought altogether. It was one that replaced history with a different model for the organization of experience: things that happen and their meaning.

This other model imposed meaning and order on things that happened. Thinking through paradigms, with a conception of time that elides past and present and removes all barriers between them, seeks and finds unities in complex data. At stake are [1] a conception of time different from the historical one and [2] premises on how to take the measure of time that form a legitimate alternative to those that define the foundations of the historical way of measuring time. All of this is implicit

Four. The Laws of History: Genesis Rabbah

in the exposition of Genesis as handbook of the principles that govern human events and unify the affairs of states and nations.

III. Implicit Truths

What is implicit is now fully exposed: the transformation of history into the science of society, the formulation of a monotheist theory of the affairs of nations. If for convenience' sake, we speak of the laws of history, we frame matters in a manner congruent to the governing conceptions of the Rabbinic canon. That is: how do issues of monotheism intrude, and in what way does narrative or mythic monotheism, counterpart for the social order to ontological monotheism, make its mark? Stated simply: in what way does God's unity shape thinking on the dynamism of human events: time and change? If it could be shown that rational rules manifestly governed, then the unity of history could be proved to match the unity of nature. To answer the historical question to the advantage of monotheism, the Rabbinic sages demonstrated the orderly character of history, its conformity to a few simple rules, which the Torah revealed. Then regularity, order, rationality — a single and uniform set of coherent laws would be shown to override the complexities of change. History could be made to show that there is a judge and there is judgment, a cogent plan dictated the course of events.

Events are there to be classified, generations to be linked into a common framework. To conclude, I point to the simplest demonstration that the generations are linked, so that what the ancestors do yields consequences for their heirs:

Genesis Rabbah LXXXIV:XX.
1. A. "Then Jacob tore his garments and put sackcloth upon his loins and mourned for his son many days" (Gen. 37:34):
   B. R. Phineas in the name of R. Hoshaiah: "The tribal fathers caused their father to tear his garments, and where were they paid back? In Egypt: 'And they tour their clothes' (Gen. 44:13).
   C. "Joseph caused the tribal fathers to tear their clothes. He was paid back in the case of the son of his son: 'And Joshua tore his clothes' (Josh. 7:6).
   D. "Benjamin caused the tribal fathers to tear their clothes. He was paid back in Shushan, the capital: 'Mordecai tore his clothes' (Est. 4:1).
   E. "Manasseh caused the tribal fathers to tear their clothes. He was paid back by having his inheritance divided into half, half on the other side of the Jordan, and half in the land of Canaan."

A massive claim, fully articulated in details, registers: the Rabbinic sages discovered in Torah the plan and intent of the one God for all humanity. They demonstrated the presence of that program in Scripture by defining the paramount patterns that inhered in Scripture itself, particularly in its narratives. Then individuals and nations could be shown to match, conforming to the same dynamic rule throughout. That conception of the cogency of human events, the presence of a single pattern that forms of them a statement of unities, is not the sole implicit affirmation in Genesis Rabbah, nor is it unique to that compilation any more than the argument of ontological monotheism is unique to Sifra. But it forms a primary and generative conception of the document.

5

The Laws of Society: Leviticus Rabbah

I. THE DOCUMENT AND ITS PROGRAM: RECURRENT QUESTIONS

The unity of nature and history, demonstrated in Genesis Rabbah, leaves open the question of corporate Israel: how do nature, history, *and* Israelite society join together to make a single statement in common? That would constitute the statement of monotheism realized in the unity of the natural and the social and world order. Answering that question in dialogue with the book of Leviticus, Leviticus Rabbah sets forth thirty-seven expositions concerning the Israelite social order in the context of holiness realized in the priesthood and sacrificial cult and Temple. Reaching closure at ca. 450 C.E., the document illustrated the implicit conviction that three realms correspond, nature, history, and Israelite society. All are constructed in conformity with a single pattern, present from creation. The premise governing throughout, then, invokes the rules of sanctifying the Temple and priesthood in the setting of Israel's social order, and furthermore finds a single pattern to which Temple and Israel, history and nature, conform to a single set of principles. God imposed uniform rules on the natural and the social order. Accordingly, what Sifra's composers accomplished for the unity of intellect, the authors and compilers of Leviticus Rabbah achieved for the unity of history and nature. Once more we find implicit theological norms that animate the acutely particular exegesis of Scripture.

These norms of conviction, not only conduct, permeate the successive documents, because they realize in concrete ways the logic of monotheism: a single, purposive God expresses his unitary plan through each component of reality: through creation, through universal history, through the composition of the social order of the holy people. That conviction is stated at Lev. R. XI:I.1ff., a fine example of the demonstration of the unity of all being, which reads Proverbs 9:1-4 in terms of the creation of two pairs of categories, the world and the war of Gog and Magog at the end of days, the Torah, and the tent of meeting. The composite thus treats as equivalent the beginning, creation, the end, the eschatological war, as one pair, and the Torah and the Temple, as another. The two matches are creation and end-time, Torah-study and Temple-sacrifice. All conform to the same pattern, specified at Proverbs 9:1-4. Scripture properly interpreted then yields God's plan and program for all aspects of existence.

Leviticus Rabbah XI:I

E. "That is in line with the following verse of Scripture: 'With wisdom the Lord founded the earth' (Prov. 3:19).

F. "'She has set up her seven pillars' refers to the seven days of the creation of the world, as it is said, 'For in six days the Lord made the world' Ex. 31:17).

G. "'She has slaughtered her beasts' (Prov. 9:2). 'Let the earth bring forth the living creature after its kind, [cattle]' (Gen. 1:24).

H. "'She has mixed her wine' (Prov. 9:2). 'Let the water be gathered together under the heaven' (Gen. 1:9).

I. "'She has also set her table.' 'And God said, Let the earth put forth grass bearing seed' (Gen. 1:11).

J. "'She has sent out her maids to call.' This refers to Adam and Eve.

K. "'From the highest places in the town' (Prov. 9:3). For the Holy One, blessed be he, exalted them up by calling them divinities.

L. "That is in line with the following verse of Scripture: 'And you will be like God' (Gen. 3:5).

M. "And at the climax of all of this glory: 'Whoever is simple, let him turn in here' (Prov. 9:4).

N. "They abandoned the counsel of the Holy One, blessed be he, and went and followed the counsel of the snake.

O. "On this account, 'To him who is without sense, she says (Come eat of my bread and drink of the wine I have mixed)' 'For dust you are and to dust you will return'" (Gen. 3:19).

Leviticus Rabbah XI:II

1. A. R. Jonah in the name of R. Abba bar Jeremiah interpreted (Prov. 9:1-4) to speak of the fate of Gog in the world to come.

B. "'Wisdom has built her house (Prov. 9:1) refers to the house of the sanctuary: "By wisdom is a house built" (Prov. 24:3).

C. "'She has set up her seven pillars' (Prov. 9:1). These (seven pillars) are the seven years of Gog."

E. "And those seven years for the righteous will serve as a prenuptial feast for the world to come.

F. "The mnemonic will be, 'One who joins in the prenuptial feast will join in the nuptial banquet.'

G. "'She has slaughtered her beasts' (Prov. 9:2). 'The flesh of the mighty will you eat' (Ez. 39:18).

H. "'She has mixed her wine' (Prov. 9:2). 'The blood of the princes of the earth will you drink' (Ez. 39:18).

Five. The Laws of Society: Leviticus Rabbah

I. "'She has also set her table' (Prov. 9:2). 'And you shall be filled at my table with horses and riders, (with mighty men and all kinds of warriors, says the Lord God)' (Ez. 39:20).

J. "'She has sent out her maids to call' (Prov. 9:3). This refers to Ezekiel: 'As for you, son of man, thus says the Lord God: Speak to the birds of every sort and to all beasts of the field, (Assemble, Come, gather from all sides to the sacrificial feast which I am preparing for you, a great sacrificial feast upon the mountains of Israel, and you shall eat flesh and drink blood. You shall eat the flesh of the mighty and drink the blood of the princes of the earth, or of rams, of lambs, and of goats, of bulls, all of them fatlings of Bashan. And you shall eat fat till you are filled, and drink blood till you are drunk, at the sacrificial feast which I am preparing for you. You shall be filled at my table, with horses and riders, with mighty men and all kinds of warriors, says the Lord God')" (Ez. 39:17-20).

Leviticus Rabbah XI:III

1. A. Bar Qappara interpreted (Prov. 9:1-4) to refer to the Torah:

B. "'Wisdom has built her house.' This (refers to) the Torah: 'The Lord created me at the beginning of his work, the first of his acts of old' (Prov. 8:22).

C. "'She has set up her seven pillars.' This refers to the seven scrolls of the Torah."

D. Are they not only five?

E. Bar Qappara treats the portion from the beginning of the book of Numbers, "And God spoke" (Num. 1:1) up to "And it came to pass, when the ark journeyed" (Num. 10:35) as a single book, and from that passage to, "And when it rested" (Num. 10:36) as yet another, and from that passage to the end of the scroll as yet another, so there are seven [with the book of Numbers counted as three separate scrolls].

F. "'She has slaughtered her beasts.' This refers to the penalties [specified in the Torah's law].

G. "'She has mixed her wine.' This refers to the arguments of exegesis of Scripture from such arguments as minor to major and analogy of expressions.

H. "'She has also set (RK) her table.' This refers to the rules of setting the value (RK) of persons who vow their own worth.

I. "'She has sent out her maids to call.' This refers to Israel.

J. "'From the highest places in the town.' This refers to the fact that the Holy One, blessed be he, exalted them, calling them divine: 'I said, You are god like beings and all of you are children of the most high' (Ps. 82:6).

K. "After all of this glory: 'Who is simple, let him turn in here.' They abandoned the counsel of the Holy One, blessed be he, and went and said to a calf, 'This is your god, O Israel' (Ex. 32:4).

L. "On this account: 'I say, you are gods, sons of the most high, all of you; nevertheless, you shall die like men and fall like any prince'" (Ps. 82:6-7).

Leviticus Rabbah XI:IV

1. A. R. Abba bar Kahana interpreted the cited passage to speak of the tent of meeting:
   B. "'Wisdom has built her house' refers to Bezalel: 'And I shall fill him with the spirit of God' (Ex. 31:3).
   C. "'She has set up her seven pillars.' This refers to the seven days of consecration.
   D. "That is in line with the following verse of Scripture: '(And you shall not go out from the door of the tent of meeting) for seven days, until the days of your ordination are completed' (Lev. 8:33).
   E. "'She has slaughtered her beasts.' This refers to the offerings (of consecration).
   F. "'She has mixed her wine.' This refers to the libations.
   G. "'She has also set her table.' This refers to the laying forth of the show bread on the table of the altar.
   H. "'She has set out her maids to call.' This refers to Moses.
   I. "That is in line with the following verse of Scripture: 'On the eighth day Moses called (Aaron and his sons and the elders of Israel)'" (Lev. 9:1).

The well-chosen intersecting verse imposes upon the base-verse the theme of creation, underscoring the theology of the cult as a recapitulation and celebration of the creation of the world. XI:I-IV make this explicit, in a remarkable composition. The success of the composite lies in its linking four distinct episodes, two by two, so showing the match between opposites: beginning and ending, learning and sacrifice. The unity of all being, demonstrated by the Mishnah in abstract exercises, now extends in concrete language to the realms of creation and end-time, service of God through Torah-study and through sacrifice.

The same point, the unity of the eternal verities that govern in the social order, registers in another way: matching past, present, and future. The same social laws characterize all three periods and yield the same results. So the past permits peeking into the future, the laws of the world-order linking all times, all places: if this, then that must follow. The heritage of Genesis Rabbah is recapitulated in the demonstration of the unity of history, past, present, future. That which has been is repeated in that which is and will be realized in that which will come to be. Time is unitary, the past forms a presence in the contemporary world, and the future rehearses what has already been, the whole composite of past, present, and future comprising a unitary complex — a remarkable demonstration of the meaning of monotheism for history and society:

Five. *The Laws of Society: Leviticus Rabbah* 55

Leviticus Rabbah XXVII:IV

1. A. "That which is already has been, [that which is to be already has been. God seeks that which is pursued]" (Qoh. 3:15).
   B. R. Judah and R. Nehemiah:
   C. R. Judah says, "If someone should say to you that had the first Adam not sinned and eaten from that tree, he would have lived and endured even to this very day, tell him, 'It already has been.' Elijah lives and endures forever.
   D. "'That which is to be already has been:' If someone should tell to you, it is possible that the Holy One, blessed be he, in the future is going to resurrect the dead, say to him, 'It already has been.' He has already resurrected the dead through Elijah, Elisha, and Ezekiel in the valley of Dura."
   E. R. Nehemiah says, "If someone should say to you that it is possible that to begin with the world was entirely made up of water in water, say to him, 'It already has been,' for the ocean is full of diverse water.
   F. "'That which is to be already has been:' If someone should say to you, the Holy One, blessed be he, is going to dry [the sea] up, say to him, 'It already has been.' 'And the children of Israel walked on dry land through the sea'" (Ex. 15:19).
2. A. R. Aha in the name of R. Simeon b. Halapta: "Whatever the Holy One, blessed be he, is destined to do in the age to come already has he shown to [humanity] in this world.
   B. "That he is going to resurrect the dead: he has already resurrected the dead through Elijah, Elisha, and Ezekiel.
   C. "That he is going to bring people through water on to dry land: 'When you pass through water, I am with you' (Is. 43:2). He has already brought Israel through water with Moses: 'And the children of Israel walked on dry land through the sea' (Ex. 15:19).
   D. "'And through rivers they shall not overwhelm you' (Is. 43:2). This he has already accomplished through Joshua: 'On dry land the Israelites crossed the Jordan' (Josh. 4:22).
   E. "'When you walk through fire you shall not be burned' (Is. 43:2). This he has already accomplished through Hananiah, Mishael, and Azariah.
   F. "'And the flame shall not consume you' (Is. 43:2). This he has already accomplished: 'The fire had not had any power over the bodies of those men ... no smell of fire had come upon them' (Dan. 3:27).
   G. "That God will sweeten bitter water, he has already accomplished through Moses: 'The Lord showed him a tree, and he threw it into the water, and the water became sweet' (Ex. 15:25).
   H. "That God will sweeten what is bitter through something bitter, he has already accomplished through Elisha: 'Then he went to the spring of water and threw salt into it and said, Thus says the Lord, I have made this water wholesome' (2 Kgs. 2:21).

I. "That God blesses what is little (and makes it much), he already has accomplished through Elijah and Elisha: 'For thus says the Lord, the God of Israel, "The jar of meal shall not be spent, and the cruse of oil shall not fail, (until the day that the Lord sends rain upon the earth)"' (1 Kgs. 17:14).
J. "That God visits barren women, he has already accomplished through Sarah, Rebecca, Rachel, and Hannah."
K. "'The wolf and the lamb will pasture together,' (Is. 65:25), he has already accomplished through Hezekiah: 'The wolf shall dwell with the lamb' (Is. 11:6).
L. "'And kings will be your tutor' (Is. 49:23) he has already accomplished through Daniel: 'Then the king Nebuchadnezzar fell upon his face and worshipped Daniel' (Dan. 2:46).

The uniformity of past, present, and future express the enduring principles that the one God has realized in creation and in Israel's history. The nations in history correspond to the types of uncleanness that the Torah specifies, a reworking of a familiar principle:

Leviticus Rabbah XV:IX
1. A. "A swelling (lifting up, S'T), [or eruption (SPHT) or a spot (BHRT)" (Lev. 13:2).
B. "A swelling refers to Babylonia."
H. "Eruption" (SPHT) refers to Media, which produced Haman, that wicked man, who inflamed (Media's) people like a snake, on the account of, "On your belly will you go" (Gen 3:14).
I. "Bright spot" (BHRT) refers to Greece, which publicizes (MHBRT) its (harsh) decrees, saying to Israel, "Write on the horn of an ox that you have no portion in the God of Israel."
J. "A spot of leprosy" (Lev. 13:2) refers to Edom, which originated in the strength of the old man [Isaac, who blessed Esau].
K. It was on account of the statement, "And it shall be on the skin of his body" (Lev. 13:2).

God's coherent, unitary program for creation and humanity responds in particular to the conduct of Israel. So a single, unitary thesis on Israelite affairs must come to expression.

Then what of the condition of Israel? The same rules that govern the nations govern Israel, which is punished for sin in unique ways. The point is, Israel is subject to fair rules, which produce reward for virtue and penalty for vice. Had Israel not sinned, it would never have produced the marks of uncleanness or other infirmities. Because of sin, infirmity afflicts Israelites. Uncleanness and deformity form evidence for the same thesis, which is, the physical condition of Israel responds to the moral condition of Israelite society:

Leviticus Rabbah XVIII:IV

1. A. R. Simeon b. Yohai taught, "When the Israelites stood before Mount Sinai and said, 'All that the Lord has spoken we shall do and we shall hear' (Ex. 24:7), among them there were no people afflicted with flux, no lepers, no cripples, no blind, no dumb, no deaf, no idiots, no imbeciles, no fools.
   B. "Concerning that hour Scripture says, 'You are wholly fair, my beloved, and there is no blemish in you' (Song 4:7).
   C. "When they had sinned, not many days passed before there were found among them people afflicted with flux, lepers, cripples, blind, dumb, deaf, idiots, imbeciles, and fools.
   D. "Concerning that hour what does Scripture then state? 'And they shall send out of the camp every leper and everyone afflicted with flux'" (Num. 5:2).
2. A. On what account were the Israelites declared liable for flux and leprosy?
   B. R. Honia in the name of R. Hoshiah: "It was because they maligned their great men, saying, 'So-and-so's family — what do they amount to? Aren't they just a bunch of lepers?'
   C. "This is meant to teach you that leprosy spots come only on account of gossip.
   D. "It was on that account that the Israelites became liable to suffer from flux and leprosy."
   E. R. Tanhuma said, "It was because they were maligning the ark and saying, 'That ark slays the people who carry it.'
   F. "And leprosy spots come only on account of gossip. On that account the Israelites became liable to suffer from flux and leprosy."
   G. Rabbis say, "It was on account of the calf, for it was written in that regard, 'And Moses saw the people, that it had broken out' (Ex. 32:25) — that among the people flux and leprosy had broken out.
   H. "How do we know? For it is said, 'His (the leper's) clothing will be disheveled and his hair will be broken out'" (Lev. 13:45).
   I. R. Judah b. R. Simon said, "It was on account of the complainers, for it is said, 'But at a whole month, until it comes out at your nostrils and becomes loathsome to you, (because you have rejected the Lord who is among you)'" (Num. 11:20).

The same law applies to the wicked and the righteous, the same judgment pertains. But the righteous are punished in this world, the wicked prosper now but pay the full penalty in the world to come. Strict justice governs the nations and Israel alike:

Leviticus Rabbah XXVII:I

1. A. "When a bull or sheep (or goat is born, it shall remain seven days with its mother; and from the eighth day on it shall be acceptable as an offering by fire to the Lord)" (Lev. 22:27).

B. "Your righteousness is like the mountains of God, your judgments are like the great deep; man and beast you save, O Lord" (Ps. 36:6).
C. R. Ishmael and R. Aqiba:
D. R. Ishmael says, "With the righteous, who carry out the Torah, which was given 'from the mountains of God' the Holy One, blessed be he, does righteousness 'like the mountains of God.'
E. "But with the wicked, who do not carry out the Torah, which was given 'from the mountains of God,' the Holy One, blessed be he, seeks a strict accounting, unto 'the great deep.'
F. "That is in line with the following verse of Scripture: 'Your judgments are like the great deep'" (Ps. 36:6).
G. R. Aqiba says, "All the same are these and those: the Holy One, blessed be he, seeks a strict accounting with (all of) them in accord with strict justice.
H. "He seeks a strict accounting with the righteous, collecting from them the few bad deeds that they did in this world, in order to pay them an abundant reward in the world to come.
I. "And he affords prosperity to the wicked and gives them a full reward for the minor religious duties that they successfully accomplished in this world, in order to exact a full penalty from them in the world to come."

The important principle is that attributed to Aqiba. The one God treats all persons in accord with a single standard of justice. But that yields the distinction between the righteous and the wicked. Everyone must face judgment. But justice operates: the wicked enjoy this world for a brief period, the righteous, enjoy the world to come for all eternity.

Of what principles does justice consist and how are these discerned? The Torah records facts to be ordered into encompassing generalizations. These will enjoy the standing of self-evidence, being demonstrated out of the record of Scripture. Scripture says God favors the pursued over the pursuer, and history is comprised by evidence of that fact.

Leviticus Rabbah XXVII:V
1. A. "God seeks what has been driven away" (Qoh. 3:15).
   B. R. Huna in the name of R. Joseph said, "It is always the case that 'God seeks what has been driven away' [favoring the victim].
   C. "You find when a righteous man pursues a righteous man, 'God seeks what has been driven away.'
   D. "When a wicked man pursues a wicked man, 'God seeks what has been driven away.'
   E. "All the more so when a wicked man pursues a righteous man, 'God seeks what has been driven away.'

Five. The Laws of Society: Leviticus Rabbah

    F.   "(The same principle applies) even when you come around to a case in which a righteous man pursues a wicked man, 'God seeks what has been driven away.'"

2. A.   R. Yosé b. R. Yudan in the name of R. Yosé b. R. Nehorai says, "It is always the case that the Holy One, blessed be he, demands an accounting for the blood of those who have been pursued from the hand of the pursuer.

    B.   "Abel was pursued by Cain, and God sought (an accounting for) the pursued: 'And the Lord looked (favorably) upon Abel and his meal offering' (Gen. 4:4).

    C.   "Noah was pursued by his generation, and God sought (an accounting for) the pursued: 'You and all your household shall come into the ark' (Gen. 7:1). And it says, 'For this is like the days of Noah to me, as I swore (that the waters of Noah should no more go over the earth)' (Is. 54:9).

    D.   "Abraham was pursued by Nimrod, 'and God seeks what has been driven away': 'You are the Lord, the God who chose Abram and brought him out of Ur' (Neh. 9:7).

    E.   "Isaac was pursued by Ishmael, 'and God seeks what has been driven away': 'For through Isaac will seed be called for you' (Gen. 21:12).

    F.   "Jacob was pursued by Esau, 'and God seeks what has been driven away': 'For the Lord has chosen Jacob, Israel for his prized possession' (Ps. 135:4).

    G.   "Moses was pursued by Pharaoh, 'and God seeks what has been driven away': 'Had not Moses His chosen stood in the breach before Him' (Ps. 106:23).

    H.   "David was pursued by Saul, 'and God seeks what has been driven away': 'And he chose David, his servant' (Ps. 78:70).

    I.   "Israel was pursued by the nations, 'and God seeks what has been driven away': 'And you has the Lord chosen to be a people to him' (Deut. 14:2).

    J.   "And the rule applies also to the matter of offerings. A bull is pursued by a lion, a sheep is pursued by a wolf, a goat is pursued by a leopard.

    K.   "Therefore the Holy One, blessed be he, has said, 'Do not make offerings before me from those animals that pursue, but from those that are pursued: 'When a bull, a sheep, or a goat is born'" (Lev. 22:27).

The cult thus contains within itself the social rules for Israelite conduct. But it is up to the sages to discern those rules in matching history and the natural order enshrined in the Temple rules. The bull, sheep, and goat all represent herbivores, whom God prefers (just as God had made Adam and Eve vegetarians). The lessons for Israelite conduct, meant to match nature and the social order, prove self-evident.

God imposes a single law on Israel and the nations, the righteous and the wicked. Does that mean a single fate comes to all? As Aqiba struggled with that dilemma of monotheism, so did others, and a consensus determined that God applies a single standard of justice to all, but in line with the requirements of justice and mercy favored the righteous over the wicked, and Israel that know him, over the nations that do not:

Leviticus Rabbah XVII:I

1. A. "The Lord said to Moses and Aaron, 'When you come into the land of Canaan, [which I give you for a possession, and I put a leprous disease in a house in the land of your possession, then he who owns the house shall come and tell the priest, 'There seems to me to be some sort of disease in my house']" (Lev. 14:33-34).
   B. "Truly God is good to Israel, to those who are pure in heart. (But as for me, my feet had almost stumbled, my steps had well nigh slipped, for I was envious of the arrogant, when I saw the prosperity of the wicked)" (Ps. 73:1-3).
   C. Is it possible [to suppose that God is good] to everybody?
   D. Scripture says, " ... to those who are pure in heart." These are those whose heart is pure in (doing) religious duties.
   E. "Blessed are the men whose strength is in you, in whose heart are the highways to Zion" (Ps. 84:5).
   F. Is it possible to suppose that this applies to everybody?
   G. Scripture says, " ... to those in whose heart are the highways ... " These are the ones in whose heart are paved the ways of the Torah.
   H. "Do good, O Lord, to those who are good, and to those who are upright in their hearts" (Ps. 125:4).
   I. Is it possible to suppose that this applies to everybody?
   J. Scripture says, " ... to those who are upright in their hearts."
   K. "The Lord is good, a stronghold in the day of trouble, (yea, he knows them that trust in him)" (Nah. 1:7).
   L. Is it possible to suppose that this applies to everybody?
   M. Scripture says, "He knows them that trust in him."
   N. "The Lord is good to those who wait for him" (Lam. 3:25).
   O. Is it possible to suppose that this applies to everybody?
   P. Scripture states, "To the soul that seeks him" (Lam. 3:25).
   Q. "The Lord is near to those that call on him" (Ps. 145:18).
   R. Is it possible to suppose that this applies to everybody?
   S. Scripture says, "To those that call upon him in truth" (Ps. 145:18).
   T. "Who is God like you, pardoning iniquity and passing over transgression for the remnant of his inheritance" (Mic. 7:18).
   U. Is it possible to suppose that this applies to everybody?
   V. Scripture says, "For the remnant of his inheritance."

God's uniform justice produces the result that God favors Israel over the nations, because Israel is pure in heart, by reason of the religious duties, conformity

Five. *The Laws of Society: Leviticus Rabbah* 61

to the ways of the Torah, trust in God, and other theological virtues. But does that mean that Israel differs in its essence from the pagan nations? Not at all. Israel distinguishes itself by its sanctification through obedience to the commandments, its careful realization of the teachings of the Torah.

Leviticus Rabbah V:VII

2. A. Said R. Eleazar, "The nations of the world are called a congregation, and Israel is called a congregation.
   B. "The nations of the world are called a congregation: 'For the congregation of the godless shall be desolate' (Job 15:34).
   C. "And Israel is called a congregation: 'And the elders of the congregation shall lay their hands' (Lev. 4:15).
   D. "The nations of the world are called sturdy bulls and Israel is called sturdy bulls.
   E. "The nations of the world are called sturdy bulls: 'The congregation of sturdy bulls with the calves of the peoples' (Ps. 68:31).
   F. "Israel is called sturdy bulls, as it is said, 'Listen to me, you sturdy bullish of heart' (Is. 46:13).
   G. "The nations of the world are called excellent, and Israel is called excellent.
   H. "The nations of the world are called excellent: 'You and the daughters of excellent nations' (Ex. 32:18).
   I. "Israel is called excellent: 'They are the excellent, in whom is all my delight' (Ps. 16:4).
   J. "The nations of the world are called sages, and Israel is called sages.
   K. "The nations of the world are called sages: 'And I shall wipe out sages from Edom' (Ob. 1:8).
   L. "And Israel is called sages: 'Sages store up knowledge' (Prov. 10:14).
   M. "The nations of the world are called unblemished, and Israel is called unblemished.
   N. "The nations of the world are called unblemished: 'Unblemished as are those that go down to the pit' (Prov. 1:12).
   O. "And Israel is called unblemished: 'The unblemished will inherit goodness' (Prov. 28:10).
   P. "The nations of the world are called men, and Israel is called men.
   Q. "The nations of the world are called men: 'And you men who work iniquity' (Ps. 141:4).
   R. "And Israel is called men: 'To you who are men I call' (Prov. 8:4).
   S. "The nations of the world are called righteous, and Israel is called righteous.
   T. "The nations of the world are called righteous: 'And righteous men shall judge them' (Ez. 23:45).
   U. "And Israel is called righteous: 'And your people — all of them are righteous' (Is. 60:21).

V. "The nations of the world are called mighty, and Israel is called mighty.
W. "The nations of the world are called mighty: 'Why do you boast of evil, O mighty man' (Ps. 52:3).
X. "And Israel is called mighty: 'Mighty in power, those who do his word' (Ps. 103:20).

Israel and the nations form a single genus of two species. They join together in the same social entity, a congregation, in the same metaphor, sturdy bulls, and so on. But Israel is speciated, in that it turns its traits into virtues, while the nations do not. That accounts for God's special love for Israel, his selection of Israel to receive the Torah:

Leviticus Rabbah XIII:II
1. A. R. Simeon b. Yohai opened (discourse by citing the following verse:) "'He stood and measured the earth; he looked and shook (YTR = released) the nations; [then the eternal mountains were scattered as the everlasting hills sank low. His ways were as of old]' (Hab. 3:6).
B. "The Holy One, blessed be he, took the measure of all the nations and found no nation but Israel that was truly worthy to receive the Torah.
C. "The Holy One, blessed be he, further took the measure of all generations and found no generation but the generation of the wilderness that was truly worthy to receive the Torah.
D. "The Holy One, blessed be he, further took the measure of all mountains and found no mountain but Mount Moriah that was truly worthy for the Presence of God to come to rest upon it.
E. "The Holy One, blessed be he, further took the measure of all cities and found no city but Jerusalem that was truly worthy in which to have the house of the sanctuary built.
F. "The Holy One, blessed be he, further took the measure of all mountains and found no mountain but Sinai that was truly worthy for the Torah to be given upon it.
G. "The Holy One, blessed be he, further took the measure of all lands and found no land but the Land of Israel that was truly worthy for Israel.
H. "That is in line with the following verse of Scripture: 'He stood and took the measure of the earth.'"

So the nations had their opportunity and came under consideration, but God found only Israel truly worthy to receive the Torah. Then nature attested to the same process of election, Mount Moriah, Jerusalem, Mount Sinai, the Land of Israel, all being measured and found worthy.

The document presupposes a variety of principles, not only the unity of nature and history and Israel, subject to a single set of principles, on which we have

Five. The Laws of Society: Leviticus Rabbah

focused. A broader survey of the premises awaits (section iii). But we now recognize a paramount premise among them all: Israel's social order, as much as the world of nature and history, conforms to a single body of rules, which come to particular expression in society, nature, and history. The unitary premise of Rabbinic Judaism that a single plan governs, a single purpose prevails comes to expression in all manner of details. These realize in concrete ways the high abstractions of a single, paramount theology, which is logically normative and exegetically taken to be normative.

II. TO WHOM, AND FOR WHOM, DOES THE DOCUMENT SPEAK?
PROPOSITIONS AND PREOCCUPATIONS

The preoccupation of Leviticus Rabbah focuses upon the interplay of sanctification and salvation, Temple and society. They unite here in a single statement. The laws of the book of Leviticus, focused as they are on the sanctification of the nation through its cult, in Leviticus Rabbah indicate the rules of corporate salvation as well. The message of Leviticus Rabbah attaches itself to the book of Leviticus, as if that book had come from prophecy and addressed the issue of the meaning of history and Israel's salvation. But the book of Leviticus came from the priesthood and spoke of sanctification. The paradoxical syllogism — the as-if reading, the opposite of how things seem — of the composers of Leviticus Rabbah therefore reaches simple formulation. In the very setting of sanctification we find the promise of salvation. In the topics of the cult and the priesthood we uncover the national and social issues of the moral life and redemptive hope of Israel. The repeated comparison and contrast of priesthood and prophecy, sanctification and salvation, turn out to produce a complement, which comes to most perfect union in the text at hand.

The focus of Leviticus Rabbah and its laws of history is upon the society of Israel, its national fate and moral condition. Indeed, nearly all of the *parashiyyot* of Leviticus Rabbah turn out to deal with the national, social condition of Israel, and this in three contexts: (1) Israel's setting in the history of the nations, (2) the sanctified character of the inner life of Israel itself, (3) the future, salvific history of Israel. So the biblical book that deals with the tabernacle, identified by the sages as the holy Temple, now is shown to address the holy people. Leviticus really discusses not the consecration of the cult but the sanctification of the nation — its conformity to God's will laid forth in the Torah, and God's rules. So when we review the document as a whole and ask what is that something else that the base text of Leviticus is supposed to address, it turns out that the sanctification of the cult stands for the salvation of the nation. So the nation now is like the cult then, the ordinary Israelite now like the priest then. The holy way of life lived now, through acts to which merit accrues, corresponds to the holy rites then.

III. IMPLICIT TRUTHS

The recurrent message of the document, implicit throughout, explicit here and there, may be stated in brief way. God loves Israel, so gave them the Torah, which defines their life and governs their welfare. Israel is alone in its category (*sui generis*), so what is a virtue to Israel is a vice to the nations, life-giving to Israel, poison to the gentiles. True, Israel sins, but God forgives that sin, having punished the nation on account of it. Such a process has yet to come to an end, but it will culminate in Israel's complete regeneration. Meanwhile, Israel's assurance of God's love lies in the many expressions of special concern, for even the humblest and most ordinary aspects of the national life: the food the nation eats, the sexual practices by which it procreates. These life-sustaining, life-transmitting activities draw God's special interest, as a mark of his general love for Israel. Israel then is supposed to achieve its life in conformity with the marks of God's love.

These indications moreover signify also the character of Israel's difficulty, namely, subordination to the nations in general, but to the fourth kingdom, Rome, in particular. Both food laws and skin diseases stand for the nations. There is yet another category of sin, also collective and generative of collective punishment, and that is social. The moral character of Israel's life, the treatment of people by one another, the practice of gossip and small-scale thuggery — these too draw down divine penalty. The nation's fate therefore corresponds to its moral condition. The moral condition, however, emerges not only from the current generation. Israel's richest hope lies in the merit of the ancestors, thus in the Scriptural record of the merits attained by the founders of the nation, those who originally brought it into being and gave it life.

The world to come will right all presently unbalanced relationships. What is good will go forward, what is bad will come to an end. The simple message is that the things people revere, the cult and its majestic course through the year, will go on; Jerusalem will come back, so too the Temple, in all their glory. Israel will be saved through the merit of the ancestors, atonement, study of Torah, practice of religious duties. The prevalence of the eschatological dimension in the formal structures, with its messianic and other expressions, here finds its counterpart in the repetition of the same few symbols in the expression of doctrine.

The theme of the moral life of Israel produces propositions concerning not only the individual but, more important, the social virtues that the community as a whole must exhibit. First of all, the message to the individual constitutes a revision, for this context, of the address to the nation: humility as against arrogance, obedience as against sin, constant concern not to follow one's natural inclination to do evil or to overcome the natural limitations of the human condition. Israel must accept its fate, obey and rely on the merits accrued through the ages and God's special love. The individual must conform, in ordinary affairs, to this same paradigm of patience and submission. Great men and women, that is, individual heroes within

Five. The Laws of Society: Leviticus Rabbah

the established paradigm, conform to that same pattern, exemplifying the national virtues. Among these Moses stands out; he has no equal. The special position of the humble Moses is complemented by the patriarchs and by David, all of whom knew how to please God and left as an inheritance to Israel the merit they had thereby attained.

If we now ask about further recurring themes or topics, there is one so commonplace that we should have to refer to the majority of paragraphs of discourse in order to provide a complete catalogue. It is the list of events in Israel's history, meaning, in this context, Israel's history solely in scriptural times, down through the return to Zion. The one-time events of the generation of the flood, Sodom and Gomorrah, the patriarchs and the sojourn in Egypt, the exodus, the revelation of the Torah at Sinai, the golden calf, the Davidic monarchy and the building of the Temple, Sennacherib, Hezekiah, and the destruction of northern Israel, Nebuchadnezzar and the destruction of the Temple in 586, the life of Israel in Babylonian captivity, Daniel and his associates, Mordecai and Haman — these events occur over and over again. They turn out to serve as paradigms of sin and atonement, steadfastness and divine intervention, and equivalent lessons.

We find, in fact, a fairly standard repertoire of scriptural heroes or villains, on the one side, and conventional lists of Israel's enemies and their actions and downfall, on the other. The boastful, for instance, include the generation of the flood, Sodom and Gomorrah, Pharaoh, Sisera, Sennacherib, Nebuchadnezzar, the wicked empire (Rome) — contrasted to Israel, "despised and humble in this world." The four kingdoms recur again and again, always ending, , with Rome, with the repeated message that after Rome will come Israel. But Israel has to make this happen through its faith and submission to God's will. Lists of enemies ring the changes on Cain, the Sodomites, Pharaoh, Sennacherib, Nebuchadnezzar, Haman.

The implicit premise of Leviticus Rabbah proves blatant. Israel is God's special love. That love is shown in a simple way. Israel's present condition of subordination derives from its own deeds. It follows that God cares, so Israel may look forward to redemption on God's part in response to Israel's own regeneration through repentance. When the exegetes proceeded to open the scroll of Leviticus, they found numerous occasions to state that proposition in concrete terms and specific contexts. The sinner brings on his own sickness. But God heals through that very ailment. The nations of the world govern in heavy succession, but Israel's lack of faith guaranteed their rule and Israel's moment of renewal will end gentile rule. Israel's leaders — priests, prophets, kings — fall into an entirely different category from those of the nations, as much as does Israel. In these and other concrete allegations, the same classical message comes forth. Israel's sorry condition in no way testifies to Israel's true worth. Leviticus Rabbah bears in its wake a continuator-document, which adds an important point to the creed laid out here: the marks of Israel's sanctification, its holy way of life, correspond to the condition of heaven. So not only history, but the heavens give testimony to the holiness of Israel, as we shall now see.

6

The Celestial Laws: Pesiqta deRab Kahana

I. THE DOCUMENT AND ITS PROGRAM: RECURRENT QUESTIONS

Pesiqta deRab Kahana forms a theological statement that the course of Israel on earth embodies the course of the moon and the solar seasons in heaven, and when Israel mends its way, all of astral nature will respond. All else forms a commentary and is comprised by details.

Leviticus Rabbah rests on the premise that a single coherent body of laws imposes upon the facts of nature and history order and purpose. An established dogma, therefore, holds that a uniform principle governs Israel's and the nations' destinies. That is another way of stating, one unique God rules human affairs, the social order, and the order of nature. But what of the realm of heaven? Do the stars in their courses move in accordance with that same purposive will that guides affairs on earth, or are there two domains, one in heaven, one on earth? What evidence does Scripture yield for the proposition, in the language of the Qaddish-prayer, "He who brings harmony [peace] to his heights [of heaven] will bring harmony for us and for all Israel"? That is the logical next question for the unfolding sequence of canonical documents to address.

The answer surfaces in the design of Pesiqta deRab Kahana. That compilation continues the approach and forms of Leviticus Rabbah (even sharing five entire chapters, borrowed by Pesiqta deRab Kahana from Leviticus Rabbah). But, moving beyond the position outlined in Leviticus Rabbah, Pesiqta deRab Kahana is so organized as to correlate the generative narratives of Israel's existence with the passage of the seasons. What happens on earth, to Israel, matches the movement of the moon and the stars in the heavens. God governs both realms, which are linked in celestial harmony. The document shows that fact by organizing its lectionary cycle so as to link the Israelite social order in history with the movement of the sun and stars in the heavens. The changing seasons, from rainy to dry, fecund to desiccated, match the axial events in the Israelite narrative, from before Passover, the first full moon beyond the vernal equinox, to the ninth of Ab and beyond, culminating in the penitential season of renewal with its climax at Tabernacles, the first full moon after the autumnal equinox.

That correlation of events with the passage of the solar seasons makes the point that the stars in the heavens respond, at God's behest, to Israel's conduct. The nexus of heaven and earth is the Temple, God's residence on earth corresponding to the heavenly throne. This point registers both in the organization of the document and its program and in specific allegations to that same effect. First we review the former, then briefly survey high points of the latter.

To understand what is remarkable in Pesiqta deRab Kahana, we have to recall two facts. First, the synagogue lections of the Pentateuch follow the narrative from Genesis through Deuteronomy. These follow a cycle that ignores the changing of the seasons. In addition, second, special lections mark special occasions, the advent of celebrations of events in Israelite history for example: the Exodus from Egypt, the giving of the Torah, the destruction of the Temple and the like. Now, the text that governs the organization of Pesiqta deRab Kahana comprises a liturgical occasion of the synagogue, which is identical to a holy day, has told our authorship what topic it wishes to take up — and therefore also what verses of Scripture (if any) prove suitable to that topic and its exposition. And the propositions for the lectionary Sabbaths correspond with the passage of the solar seasons, spring and the end of the rainy season with Passover, fall and the start of the rainy season with Tabernacles, for example.

Adar-Nisan-Sivan
    Passover-Pentecost: *Pisqaot* 2-12
Tammuz-Ab-Elul
    The Ninth of Ab: *Pisqaot* 13-22
Tishré
    Tishré 1-22: *Pisqaot* 23-28

The twenty-eight *pisqa'ot* of Pesiqta deRab Kahana in order follow the synagogal lections from early spring through fall, in the Western calendar, from late February or early March through late September or early October, approximately half of the solar year, 27 weeks, and somewhat more than half of the lunar year. On the very surface, the basic building block is the theme of a given lectionary Sabbath — that is, a special occasion distinguished by a particular lection. The topical program of the document may be defined very simply: expositions of themes dictated by special Sabbaths or festivals and their lections.

Six. The Celestial Laws: Pesiqta deRab Kahana

PISQA	BASE-VERSE	TOPIC OR OCCASION
1.	*On the day Moses completed* (Num. 7:1)	Torah-lection for the Sabbath of Hanukkah
2.	*When you take the census* (Ex. 30:12)	Torah-lection for the Sabbath of Sheqalim first of the four Sabbaths prior to the advent of Nisan, in which Passover falls
3.	*Remember Amalek* (Deut. 25:17-19)	Torah-lection for the Sabbath of Zakhor second of the four Sabbaths prior to the advent of Nisan, in which Passover falls
4.	*Red heifer* (Num. 19:1ff.)	Torah-lection for the Sabbath of Parah third of the four Sabbaths prior to the advent of Nisan, in which Passover falls
5.	*This month* (Ex. 12:1-2)	Torah-lection for the Sabbath of Hahodesh fourth of the four Sabbaths prior to the advent of Nisan, in which Passover falls
6.	*My offerings* (Num. 28:1-4)	Torah-lection for the New Moon which falls on a weekday
7.	*It came to pass at midnight* (Ex. 12:29-32)	Torah-lection for the first day of Passover
8.	*The first sheaf* (Lev. 23:11)	Torah-lection for the second day of Passover on which the first sheaves of barley were harvested and waved as an offering
9.	*When a bull or sheep or goat is born* (Lev. 22:26)	Lection for Passover
10.	*You shall set aside a tithe* (Deut. 14:22)	Torah-lection for Sabbath during Passover in the Land of Israel or for the eighth day of Passover outside of the Land of Israel
11.	*When Pharaoh let the people go* (Ex. 13:17-18)	Torah-lection for the Seventh Day of Passover
12.	*In the third month* (Ex. 19:1ff.)	Torah-lection for Pentecost
13.	*The words of Jeremiah* (Jer. 1:1-3)	Prophetic lection for the first of three Sabbaths prior to the Ninth of Ab

Pisqa	Base-verse	Topic or Occasion
14.	*Hear* (Jer. 2:4-6)	Prophetic lection for the second of three Sabbaths prior to the Ninth of Ab
15.	*How lonely sits the city* (Lam. 1:1-2)	Prophetic lection for the third of three Sabbaths prior to the Ninth of Ab
16.	*Comfort* (Is. 40:1-2)	Prophetic lection for the first of seven Sabbaths following the Ninth of Ab
17.	*But Zion said* (Is. 49:14-16)	Prophetic lection for the second of seven Sabbaths following the Ninth of Ab
18.	*O afflicted one, storm tossed* (Is. 54:11-14)	Prophetic lection for the third of seven Sabbaths following the Ninth of Ab
19.	*I even I am he who comforts you* (Is. 51:12-15)	Prophetic lection for the fourth of seven Sabbaths following the Ninth of Ab
20.	*Sing aloud, O barren woman* (Is. 54:1ff.)	Prophetic lection for the fifth of seven Sabbaths following the Ninth of Ab
21.	*Arise, Shine* (Is. 60:1-3)	Prophetic lection for the sixth of seven Sabbaths following the Ninth of Ab
22.	*I will greatly rejoice in the Lord* (Is. 61:10-11)	Prophetic lection for the seventh of seven Sabbaths following the Ninth of Ab
23.	*The New Year*	No base verse indicated. The theme is God's justice and judgment.
24.	*Return O Israel to the Lord your God* (Hos. 14:1-3)	Prophetic lection for the Sabbath of Repentance between New Year and Day of Atonement
25.	*Selihot*	No base verse indicated. The theme is God's forgiveness.
26.	*After the death of the two sons of Aaron* (Lev. 16:1ff.)	Torah-lection for the Day of Atonement
27.	*And you shall take on the first day* (Lev. 23:39-43)	Torah-lection for the first day of the Festival of Tabernacles
28.	*On the eighth day* (Num. 29:35-39)	Torah-lection for the Eighth Day of Solemn Assembly

Six. The Celestial Laws: Pesiqta deRab Kahana

The twenty-eight *pisqa'ot* set forth propositions in the manner of the authorship of Leviticus Rabbah. But these are framed by appeal not only to the rules governing the holy society, as in Leviticus Rabbah, but also to the principal events of Israel's history, celebrated in the worship of the synagogue. And that carries us to the main point. The movement of the solar seasons correlates with the specified events, the rainy season from Tabernacles through Passover, celebrating Israel's exodus from Egypt, dwelling in the wilderness, dedication of the Temple, the dry season commemorating the siege and fall of Jerusalem, three Sabbaths of gloom from the siege to the fall, then seven Sabbaths of consolation, leading up to the season of judgment and forgiveness of Elul and Tishré. Nature responds to Israel's condition, the celestial laws with those of mankind on earth.

That brings us to explicit statements that Israel's axiological events are marked by the passage of the seasons, stated more broadly, that heaven and earth meet in the sacred life of Israel, at the Temple, the nexus of earthly nature and celestial supernature, for example.

Pesiqta deRab Kahana XXI:I
1. A. "Therefore let the Lord be glorified in the regions of the east, [and the name of the Lord the God of Israel in the coasts and islands of the west]" (Is. 24:15):
   B. [Interpreting the word for regions of the east in its literal sense, lights:] with what do people honor him?
   C. With lights.
   D. R. Abbahu said, "With two lights: 'And God made the two great lights' (Gen. 1:16).
   E. "How so? When the sun shines, people recite a blessing over it. When the moon comes out, people make a blessing over it."
   F. And rabbis say, "Said the Holy One, blessed be He, to Israel, 'My children, since my light is your light and your light is my light, let us – both you and I – together go and give light to Zion:
   G. "'Arise, shine, [for your light has come, and the glory of the Lord has risen upon you. For behold, darkness shall cover the earth, and thick darkness the peoples; but the Lord will arise upon you and his glory will be seen upon you. And nations shall come to your light, and kings to the brightness of your rising] (Isaiah 60:1-3).'"

Here is how nature and supernature, earth and heaven, correlate and make a harmonious statement. Israel responds to the sun and the moon, reciting blessings at sunrise and sunset for the sun, at the advent of the new moon for the moon. These form statements of honor of God, the creator of the lights in the heavens. And the match is the light afforded to Zion. Israel's illumination matches Heaven's.

The point at which the celestial meets the earthly is the Temple in Jerusalem, which replicates the heavenly light:

Pesiqta deRab Kahana XXVII:II

3. A. "You show me the path of life, [in your presence there is fullness of joy"] (Ps. 16:11).
   B. Read not fullness (SWB') but seven (SB'). These are the seven groups of righteous men who are going to receive the face of the Presence of God.
   C. And their face is like the sun, moon, firmament, lightning, stars, lilies, and the candelabrum that was in the house of the sanctuary.
   D. How do we know that it is like the sun? As it is said, "Clear as the sun" (Song 6:10).
   E. How do we know that it is like the moon? As it is said, "As lovely as the moon" (Song 6:10).
   F. How do we know that it is like the firmament? As it is said, "And they that are wise shall shine as the brightness of the firmament" (Dan. 12:3).
   G. How do we know that it is like the lightning? As it is said, "Their appearance is like torches, they run to and fro like lightning" (Nah. 2:5).
   H. And how do we know that it is like the stars? As it is said, "And they that turn the many to righteousness as the stars forever and ever" (Dan. 12:3).
   I. How do we know that it is like lilies? As it is said, "For the leader: upon the lilies" (Ps. 69:1).
   J. How do we know that it will be like the candelabrum of the house of the sanctuary? As it is said, "And he said to me, 'What do you see?' And I said, 'I looked and behold [there was] a candelabrum all of gold'" (Zech. 4:2).

The groups of the righteous are illuminated like the sun, moon, firmament, lightning, stars, lilies, and the Temple candelabrum. The motif of light comes to the fore time and again, with special reference to the end of days and the conditions prevailing then. God will then afford illumination for Israel, as the Temple sanctuary does even now:

Pesiqta deRab Kahana XXI:V

2. A. R. Samuel bar Nahman: "While in this age people go by day in the light of the sun and by night in the light of the moon, in the coming age, they will undertake to go only by the light of the sun by day, and not by the light of the moon by night.
   B. "What verse of Scripture indicates it? 'The sun shall no longer be your light by day, nor the moon shine on you when evening falls; [the Lord shall be your everlasting light, your God shall be your glory. Never again shall your sun set, nor your moon withdraw her light; but the Lord shall be your everlasting light and the days of your mourning shall be ended]' (Is. 60:19-20).

Six. The Celestial Laws: Pesiqta deRab Kahana

C. "By what light will they walk? By the light of the Holy One, blessed be He, in line with the passage: 'the Lord shall be your everlasting light.'"

God will bring light from heaven to illuminate the nights of the age to come. Now we turn to the illumination emanating from the Temple:

Pesiqta deRab Kahana XXI:V

3. A. Said R. Haninah, "There were windows in the house of the sanctuary, from which light shown outward into the world.
   B. "That is in line with the following verse of Scripture: 'He made for the house windows that were broad and narrow' (1 Kgs. 6:4).
   C. "They were transparent and opaque, narrow on the inside and broad on the outside, so as to draw the light outward into the world."
4. A. Said R. Levi, "Under ordinary circumstances when someone builds a palace, he makes the windows so that they are narrow on the outside and broad on the inside, so as to bring the light inside.
   B. "But the windows of the house of the sanctuary were not that way. Rather they were narrow on the inside and broad on the outside, so as to draw the light outward into the world."
5. A. R. Berekhiah in the name of R. Besallah: "It is written, 'And there were windows round about in it [and in its vestibule like the windows of the others]' (Ez. 40:25).
   B. "It is not written, 'Like this window,' but rather, like the windows of the others. They were dim and opaque, narrow on the inside and broad on the outside, so as to draw the light outward into the world."

The Temple on earth corresponds to the sun and the moon in heaven. And, at the climax of the composition, when did light go forth and how? God cloaked himself in light as in a garment and that formed the source of light for the world:

Pesiqta deRab Kahana XXI:V

6. A. R. Simeon b. Yehosedeq sent and asked R. Samuel b. Nahman, "Since I have heard that you are a master of lore, [I ask you this question:] When did the light go forth into the world?"
   B. He said to him, "The Holy One, blessed be He, cloaked himself in it as in a white garment and illuminated the entire world from the splendor of his glory."
   C. He said this to him in a whisper [as if it were a teaching of dubious authority].
   D. He said to him, "That is, in point of fact, a well-known verse of Scripture: 'Who covers yourself with light as with a garment' (Ps. 104:2), so why do you repeat this to me in a whisper?"
   E. He said to him, "Just as others told it to me in a whisper, so I repeat it to you in a whisper. And if it were not for the fact that R. Isaac had expounded the same matter in public, it would not be permitted to repeat it at all."

F. Before that time what did people say?
G. Said R. Berekhiah, "From the place of the house of the sanctuary light went forth to the world.
H. "That is in line with the following verse of Scripture: 'And behold, the glory of the God of Israel came from the east and the sound of his coming was like the sound of many waters, and the earth shone with his glory' (Ez. 43:2).
I. "The word glory refers only to the house of the sanctuary, in line with this verse: 'You throne of glory on high from the beginning, you place of our sanctuary' (Jer. 17:12)."

Light from the heavens emanates from God. God dwelt on earth but gradually departed, step by step, for the Heavens, where he was domiciled until the destruction of the Temple, at which point he resumed residence in heaven. Here is where we find the most explicit statement of the correlation of heaven and earth: God came down to earth and dwelt among men, then he left the earth and took up residence in heaven. There were seven layers of the firmament, and God resided at the lowest, with man, until Adam sinned, when he went up to the first firmament, and so through to the seventh. But righteous men brought the residence back to earth.

Pesiqta deRab Kahana I:I.
3. A. R. Tanhum, son-in-law of R. Eleazar b. Abina, in the name of R. Simeon b. Yosni: "What is written is not, 'I have come into the garden,' but rather, I have come back to my garden. That is, 'to my canopy.'
B. "That is to say, to the place in which the principal [presence of God] had been located to begin with.
C. "The principal locale of God's presence had been among the lower creatures, in line with this verse: And they heard the sound of the Lord God walking about (Gen. 3:8)."
6. A. [Reverting to 3.C,] the principal locale of God's presence had been among the lower creatures, but when the first man sinned, it went up to the first firmament.
B. The generation of Enosh came along and sinned, and it went up from the first to the second.
C. The generation of the flood [came along and sinned], and it went up from the second to the third.
D. The generation of the dispersion [came along] and sinned, and it went up from the third to the fourth.
E. The Egyptians in the time of Abraham our father [came along] and sinned, and it went up from the fourth to the fifth.
F. The Sodomites [came along], and sinned, ...from the fifth to the sixth.

Six. The Celestial Laws: Pesiqta deRab Kahana

G. The Egyptians in the time of Moses...from the sixth to the seventh.
H. And, corresponding to them, seven righteous men came along and brought it back down to earth:
I. Abraham our father came along and acquired merit, and brought it down from the seventh to the sixth.
J. Isaac came along and acquired merit and brought it down from the sixth to the fifth.
K. Jacob came along and acquired merit and brought it down from the fifth to the fourth.
L. Levi came along and acquired merit and brought it down from the fourth to the third.
M. Kehath came along and acquired merit and brought it down from the third to the second.
N. Amram came along and acquired merit and brought it down from the second to the first.
O. Moses came along and acquired merit and brought it down to earth.
P. Therefore it is said, "On the day that Moses completed the setting up of the Tabernacle, he anointed and consecrated it" (Num. 7:1).

There are some chronological curiosities, with God's departure intersecting with God's restoration. But the main point is clear. The same story is continued in the following, which traces God's departure from the Temple to the firmament:

Pesiqta deRab Kahana XIII:XI

1. A. Another matter concerning "The words of Jeremiah:"
B. The name [referring to the letters r m y h] means, the Lord went up.
2. A. In ten upward stages the Presence of God departed: from the cherub to the cherub, from the cherub to the threshold of the temple-building; from the threshold of the temple to the two cherubim; from the two cherubim to the eastern gate of the sanctuary; from the eastern gate of the sanctuary to the [wall of the] temple court; from the [wall of the] temple court to the altar; from the altar to the roof; from the roof to the city wall, from the city wall to the city, from the city to the Mount of Olives.
B. ...from the ark cover to the cherub: "And he rode upon a cherub and flew" (2 Sam. 22:11).
C. ...from the cherub to the cherub: "And the glory of the Lord mounted up from the cherub to the threshold of the house" (Ez. 10:45).
D. ...from the threshold of the temple to the two cherubim: "And the glory of the Lord went forth from off the threshold of the house and stood over the cherubim" (Ez. 10:18). Lo, it was necessary to say only, And the glory of the Lord came...
E. They drew a parable: to what may the matter be compared? To the case of a king who was leaving his palace. He kissed the walls and

embraced the columns and said, "May you remain whole, O my house, may you remain whole, O my palace." So the Presence of God kissed the walls and embraced the columns and said, "May you remain whole, O my house, may you remain whole, O my palace."

F. ...from the two cherubim to the eastern gate of the sanctuary: "The cherubs raised their wings and flew above the earth before my eyes" (Ez. 10:9).

G. ...from the eastern gate of the sanctuary to the [wall of the] temple court: "And the courtyard was filled with the splendor of the glory of the Lord" (Ez. 10:4).

H. ...from the [wall of the temple] court to the altar: "I saw the Lord standing beside the altar" (Amos 9:1).

I. ...from the altar to the roof: "It is better to dwell on the corner of the roof" (Prov. 21:9).

J. ...from the roof to the city wall: "Lo, he showed me, and behold, the Lord was standing on the wall made by a plumb line" (Amos 7:7).

K. ...from the city wall to the city: A voice cries, "The Lord into the city" (Mic. 6:9).

L. ...from the city to the Mount of Olives: "And the glory of the Lord went up from the midst of the city and stood on the mountain" (Ez. 11:23).

3. A. Said R. Jonathan, "For three and a half years the Presence of God stayed on the Mount of Olives, declaring three times a day, saying, 'Return, wandering children, I shall heal your back-slidings' (Jer. 3:22).

B. "But when they did not repent, the Presence of God began to fly in the air, reciting this verse of Scripture: 'I will go and return to my place until they confess their guilt and seek my face, in their trouble they will seek me earnestly' (Hos. 5:15)."

The premise throughout is self-evident: Heaven and earth correlate, and God rules in both domains. The same laws that apply down here apply up there, and God brings harmony between heaven and earth. When Israel complies with the Torah, God resides on earth, in the Temple. When Israel sins, God changes his abode. But wherever God locates his presence, God rules heaven and earth. That position, stated explicitly, generates the specific propositions of the lectionary cycle corresponding with the solar seasons and matching key-chapters in Israel's history.

II. TO WHOM, AND FOR WHOM, DOES THE DOCUMENT SPEAK? PROPOSITIONS AND PREOCCUPATIONS

The implicit issue of Pesiqta deRab Kahana concerns astrology, regarded in antiquity as an exact science. Is Israel subject to planetary influence, in which

Six. The Celestial Laws: Pesiqta deRab Kahana

case God's rule is compromised, or is Israel solely subject to the covenant with God? The document before us speaks for the main stream of Rabbinic opinion in insisting that God rules in heaven as much as on earth, and Israel is subject to God's will, dictated by the condition of the covenant, and not to the movement of the stars in the heavens. The answer is expressed in the very concept, the kingdom of Heaven, and the yoke of the kingdom of heaven, meaning, the rule of God and the expression of that rule in the commandments. Israel on earth is governed from heaven, but that is by God, not by the stars.

The synagogue through the paramount Torah-cycle of lections in succession calls Israel to rehearse, week by week, the chapters of Israel's formative life: Genesis for the foundation of Israel, Exodus through Numbers, then Deuteronomy, for the definition of Israel. Then, on a given week, Israel once more recapitulates through its paradigmatic and definitive narrative the earthly story of itself. This week the world was made, that week recalls the Flood, the next, the call to Abraham, and so throughout. So through the lectionary cycle the past is made present, the present resituated in the past, historical time, marked by unique, one-time events, is recapitulated, the past both recognized and renewed.

In that context Pesiqta deRab Kahana has made a remarkable choice. It is to impose upon the story of Israel's formation and definition another dimension, another layer of being: the heavenly. It is now Israel in the context — indeed, in control — of natural time, marked by the stars and the seasons. The Sabbaths of Joseph's story, for example, that in the annual lectionary cycle come in Kislev in accord with the annual cycle of lections, as the contents of Pesiqta de Rab Kahana have shown us above, embody also the occasion of the rededication of the Temple. *But these do not intersect.*

Implicit in every *Pisqa'*, then is the intent to highlight Israel as the counterpart, on earth, to the heavenly bodies. And, as I stress, the unfolding of Israelite existence on earth, the patterns of its relationship with God — these correspond down here to the movement of the moon and sun in the heavens above. But though taken with that correlation, we should not miss the point: the stars in their courses respond to Israel's conduct. The cycle of time as told by Pesiqta deRab Kahana treats Israel not as a principal player in world history on earth alone, as does the Pentateuchal cycle as framed by the Rabbinic masters. Rather, astral Israel now represents a cosmic presence, a heavenly actor on the natural stage of the Temple, along with the moon in relationship to the sun and the passage of the natural seasons.

Israel is not subject to astral influence because Israel forms a celestial body. Discerning in its activities the recurrent pattern of the skies, Pesiqta deRab Kahana substitutes theology for astrology. Then, along with the Bavli's famous composite, "Israel is not subject to planetary influences" (Bavli Shabbat 152b-153a) it forms a kind of anti-astrology, one might say. That is because the message throughout is, Israel makes choices and bears responsibility for those choices. So it relates to the movement of the moon and the sun through the seven levels of heaven signified by the fixed stars. But this is not in the way in which others are subject to the same heavenly movements. Israel drives its own chariot through the skies, the nations are merely passengers on a chariot that for their part they do not drive.

III. IMPLICIT TRUTHS

The match of terrestrial and celestial realms, the whole in cosmic harmony, implicit in the construction of the document and its program, comes to articulate expression only occasionally. But the document throughout takes for granted and affirms a wide variety of familiar theological data. These synagogal discourses, read in their entirety, form a coherent statement of three propositions, which forms norms everywhere affirmed:

[1] God loves Israel, that love is unconditional, and Israel's response to God must be obedience to the religious duties that God has assigned, which will produce merit. Israel's obedience to God is what will save Israel. That means doing the religious duties as required by the Torah, which is the mark of God's love for — and regeneration of — Israel. The tabernacle symbolizes the union of Israel and God. When Israel does what God asks above, Israel will prosper down below. If Israel remembers Amalek down below, God will remember Amalek up above and will wipe him out. A mark of Israel's loyalty to God is remembering Amalek. God does not require the animals that are sacrificed, since man could never match God's appetite, if that were the issue, but the savor pleases God as a mark of Israel's loyalty and obedience. The first sheaf returns to God God's fair share of the gifts that God bestows on Israel, and those who give it benefit, while those who hold it back suffer. Observing religious duties, typified by the rites of Tabernacles, called simply The Festival, brings a great reward of that merit that ultimately leads to redemption. God's ways are just, righteous and merciful, as shown by God's concern that the offspring remain with the mother for seven days. God's love for Israel is so intense that he wants to hold them back for an extra day after The Festival in order to spend more time with them, because, unlike the nations of the world, Israel knows how to please God. This is a mark of God's love for Israel.

[2] God is reasonable and when Israel has been punished, it is in accord with God's rules. God forgives penitent Israel and is abundant in mercy. Laughter is vain because it is mixed with grief. A wise person will not expect too much joy. But when people suffer, there ordinarily is a good reason for it. That is only one sign that God is reasonable and that God never did anything lawless and wrong to Israel or made unreasonable demands, and there was, therefore, no reason for Israel to lose confidence in God or to abandon him. God punished Israel to be sure. But this was done with reason. Nothing happened to Israel of which God did not give fair warning in advance, and Israel's failure to heed the prophets brought about her fall. And God will forgive a faithful Israel. Even though the Israelites sinned by

Six. The Celestial Laws: Pesiqta deRab Kahana

making the golden calf, God forgave them and raised them up. On the New Year, God executes justice, but the justice is tempered with mercy. The rites of the New Year bring about divine judgment and also forgiveness because of the merit of the fathers. Israel must repent and return to the Lord, who is merciful and will forgive them for their sins. The penitential season of the New Year and Day of Atonement is the right time for confession and penitence, and God is sure to accept penitence. By exercising his power of mercy, the already-merciful God grows still stronger in mercy.

[3] God will save Israel personally at a time and circumstance of his own choosing. Israel may know what the future redemption will be like, because of the redemption from Egypt. The paradox of the red cow, that what imparts uncleanness, namely touching the ashes of the red cow, produces cleanness, is part of God's ineffable wisdom, which man cannot fathom. Only God can know the precise moment of Israel's redemption. That is something man cannot find out on his own. But God will certainly fulfill the predictions of the prophets about Israel's coming redemption. The Exodus from Egypt is the paradigm of the coming redemption. Israel has lost Eden — but can come home, and, with God's help, will. God's unique power is shown through Israel's unique suffering. In God's own time, he will redeem Israel.

To develop this point, the authorship proceeds to further facts, worked out in its propositional discourses. The lunar calendar, particular to Israel, marks Israel as favored by God, for the new moon signals the coming of Israel's redemption, and the particular new moon that will mark the actual event is that of Nisan. When God chooses to redeem Israel, Israel's enemies will have no power to stop him, because God will force Israel's enemies to serve Israel, because of Israel's purity and loyalty to God. Israel's enemies are punished, and what they propose to do to Israel, God does to them. Both directly and through the prophets, God is the source of true comfort, which he will bring to Israel.

Israel thinks that God has forsaken them. But it is Israel who forsook God, God's love has never failed, and will never fail. Even though he has been angry, his mercy still is near and God has the power and will to save Israel. God has designated the godly for himself and has already promised to redeem them. He will assuredly do so. God personally is the one who will comfort Israel. While Israel says there is no comfort, in fact, God will comfort Israel. Zion/Israel is like a barren woman, but Zion will bring forth children, and Israel will be comforted. Both God and Israel will bring light to Zion, which will give light to the world. The rebuilding of Zion will be a source of joy for the entire world, not for Israel alone. God will rejoice in Israel, Israel in God, like bride and groom.

Pesiqta deRab Kahana takes an essential role in the larger theological program of Rabbinic Judaism. This it does by superimposing, upon the Pentateuchal story of Israel's beginning, the narrative of the ending — destruction but also atonement, forgiveness, renewal, for both corporate Israel and the Israelite. The reliable heavens then guarantee what is to come about, the seasons in their sequence embody the promise of the coming redemption: consolation and restoration following repentance, atonement, and forgiveness. The summer drought, the advent of the early rains — these now are made, in the very heart of synagogue liturgy, to signify the existential reality of Israel in its encounter with God.

What makes Pesiqta deRab Kahana's revision of the lectionary encounter powerful and persuasive ought not to be missed. It is its emphasis upon the correspondence of the cycle of nature with the exemplary moments of Israel's existence, the whole abstracted from linear history. The dedication and celebration in the Temple, loss of the Temple, atonement and renewal and restoration correspond to nature's cycle. Then, after the season of desiccation and death, the renewal signified by the winter rains, comes the climax of Passover-Pentecost. Then the sequence concludes with the advent of the summer's drought, followed by renewal once more.

We should not miss the radical change represented by this reading of the cycle of nature that defines the rhythm of the Israelite year. While the lunar-solar calendar conventionally interpreted knows two climactic moments, the first full moon after the vernal equinox, then the same after the autumnal equinox, for Passover and Pentecost, respectively, Pesiqta deRab Kahana has constructed a single, continuous cyclical sequence, as I have explained. Events of nature, the unfolding of the lunar year, and events of history, the unfolding of Israel's life in historical time, are formed into a single, unitary construction. That is, furthermore, transformed into a paradigm of the life of not only corporate Israel but also the individual Israelite. Nature, Israel, the Israelite — all now are given their moment in the lectionary life of the synagogue. The norm makes its mark.

7

Knowing God: Lamentations Rabbah

i. The Document and its Program: Recurrent Questions

The question left open by the documents we have considered to this point proves blatant: how do Israel and God relate, and what defines the encounter between the one God, whose unity pervades history, nature, society, and the heavens, and the singular, unique people, Israel. Laws of intellect and logic, history, nature, and society, in heaven and earth, manifest that unity. But they do not tell how the one God of heaven and earth relates to humanity in general, or to Israel, to whom God has made himself and his purpose known in the Torah, in particular.

The canonical documents treated here and in the next chapter define that relationship through law and love. The law of the Torah governs, but God's and Israel's reciprocal love intervenes. Implicit in the relationship subject to law is that the one God stands in a covenanted relationship with Israel, binding himself to obey the stipulations of that covenant. God will respond to Israel's obedience to the covenant, and Israel's conduct governs its destiny—the relationship of covenantal nomism. But the one God transcends the covenant through freely-given love for Israel, as we shall see in Chapter Eight in the encounter with Song of Songs Rabbah. The implicit norms of covenantal nomism and a relationship of love animate the final documents in this rapid survey of the implicit normative theology of Rabbinic Judaism.

It overstates the case, however, to ask Lamentations Rabbah to attest to the implicit norm of covenantal nomism. The theme of Lamentations Rabbah, a commentary on the book of Lamentations of indeterminate date, is not principally that Israel's relationship with God is defined by the covenant. True, the message concerning that theme is that the stipulative covenant still governs, and always will govern, that relationship. Therefore everything that happens to Israel makes sense and bears meaning. But Lamentations Rabbah does not expound covenantal nomism, it rather illustrates it. That is by the exposition of the calamity of 586 B.C.E., with its doppelganger of 70 C.E., as a cataclysmic event in Israel's relationship with God. As the prophets beginning with Moses asserted, disaster comes about as punishment for Israel's corporate sin.

Accordingly, God is intimately involved in events, which embody his plan and will, made manifest in the Torah. What happens to Israel expresses the conditions of the covenant — but, Lamentations Rabbah adds, God also participates in Israel's sorrow. Thus while the document takes for granted that Israel is not helpless before its fate but by its deeds controls its own destiny, its recurrent motif is the emotional engagement between God and Israel. That engagement cannot be captured only in the doctrine of covenantal nomism. God weeps for Israel and shares in Israel's suffering. God mourns when Israel's deeds bring on disaster.

This is the one and whole message of the compilation, and it is the only message that is repeated throughout; everything else proves secondary and derivative of the fundamental proposition that the destruction of the Temple in Jerusalem in 70 C.E. — as much as in 586 B.C.E. — proves the implicit norm: God's tears in the end attest to the enduring validity of the covenant, its rules and its promise of redemption. And that sets the stage for what follows in Song of Songs Rabbah: the daring exposition of enduring love that joins Israel and God — a love beyond the covenant, a love of utter grace.

That is not to minimize the importance of the covenantal nomism, on which all else is constructed. The covenant and Israel's adherence to it make all the difference. In the following the contrast is drawn between the consequences of fulfilling the requirements of the Torah and of not doing so. These are framed in the language, "had you had the merit...," "but since you did not have the merit...," with the explicit allusion to the teaching of the Torah that could have brought blessings, if realized, but, ignored, has caused calamity.

LAMENTATIONS RABBAH XI.I.

1. A. R. Isaac commenced [by citing the following verse of Scripture]: "'Because you would not serve the Lord your God in joy and gladness over the abundance of everything, you shall have to serve in hunger and thirst, naked and lacking everything, the enemies whom the Lord will let loose against you. He will put an iron yoke upon your neck until he has wiped you out' (Dt. 28:47-48).
    B. "Had you had the merit, you would have read in the Torah: 'You will bring them in and plant them in the mountain of your inheritance' (Ex. 15:17).
    C. "But since you did not have the merit: 'Let all their wickedness come before you' (Lam. 1:22).
    D. "Had you had the merit, you would have read in the Torah: 'The peoples have heard, they tremble' (Ex. 15:14).

Seven. Knowing God: Lammentations Rabbah

E. "But since you did not have the merit: 'They have heard that I sigh' (Lam. 1:21).

F. "Had you had the merit, you would have read in the Torah: 'I have surely seen the affliction of my people that are in Egypt' (Ex. 3:7).

G. "But since you did not have the merit: 'O Lord, for I am in distress, mine innards burn' (Lam. 1:20).

H. "Had you had the merit, you would have read in the Torah: 'And you shall make proclamation on the selfsame day' (Lev. 23:21).

I. "But since you did not have the merit: 'I called for my lovers but they deceived me' (Lam. 1:19).

J. "Had you had the merit, you would have read in the Torah: 'Justice, justice you shall follow' (Dt. 16:20).

K. "But since you did not have the merit: 'The Lord is just, for I have rebelled against his word' (Lam. 1:18).

L. "Had you had the merit, you would have read in the Torah: 'You shall surely open your hand to your brother' (Dt. 15:11).

M. "But since you did not have the merit: 'Zion spreads forth her hands' (Lam. 1:17).

N. "Had you had the merit, you would have read in the Torah: 'These are the appointed seasons of the Lord' (Lev. 23:4).

O. "But since you did not have the merit: 'These things I weep' (Lam. 1:16).

P. "Had you had the merit, you would have read in the Torah: 'We will go up by the highway' (Num. 20:19).

Q. "But since you did not have the merit: 'The Lord has set at naught all my mighty men' [the word play is on highway, *messilah,* and naught, *sillah*].

R. "Had you had the merit, you would have read in the Torah: 'And I have broken the bars of your yoke' (Lev. 26:13).

S. "But since you did not have the merit: 'The yoke of my transgressions is impressed by his hand' (Lam. 1:14).

T. "Had you had the merit, you would have read in the Torah: 'Fire shall be kept burning upon the altar continually' (Lev. 6:6).

U. "But since you did not have the merit: 'From on high he has sent fire into my bones' (Lam. 1:13).

V. "Had you had the merit, you would have read in the Torah: 'In all the way that you went' (Dt. 1:31).

W. "But since you did not have the merit: 'Let it not come to you, all you that pass in the way' (Lam. 1:12).

X. "Had you had the merit, you would have read in the Torah: 'And you shall eat your bread until you have enough' (Lev. 26:5).

Y. "But since you did not have the merit: 'All her people sigh, they seek bread' (Lam. 1:11).

Z. "Had you had the merit, you would have read in the Torah: 'Neither shall any man covet your land' (Ex. 34:24).

AA. "But since you did not have the merit: 'The enemy has spread out his hand upon all her coveted treasures' (Lam. 1:10).

BB. "Had you had the merit, you would have read in the Torah: 'For on this day shall atonement be made for you to cleanse you' (Lev. 16:30).

CC. "But since you did not have the merit: 'Her filthiness was in her skirts' (Lam. 1:9).

DD. "Had you had the merit, you would have read in the Torah: 'From all your sins shall you be clean before the Lord' (Lev. 16:30).

EE. "But since you did not have the merit: 'Jerusalem has grievously sinned' (Lam. 1:8).

FF. "Had you had the merit, you would have read in the Torah: 'And you shall be remembered before the Lord your God' (Num. 10:9).

GG. "But since you did not have the merit: 'Jerusalem remembers in the days of her afflictions' (Lam. 1:7).

HH. "Had you had the merit, you would have read in the Torah: 'And I will walk among you' (Lev. 26:12).

II. "But since you did not have the merit: 'And gone is from the daughter of Zion all her splendor' (Lam. 1:6).

JJ. "Had you had the merit, you would have read in the Torah: 'And the Lord will make you the head' (Dt. 28:13).

KK. "But since you did not have the merit: 'Her adversaries are become the head, her enemies are at ease' (Lam. 1:5).

LL. "Had you had the merit, you would have read in the Torah: 'Three times a year shall all your males appear before the Lord' (Dt. 16:16).

MM. "But since you did not have the merit: 'The ways of Zion do mourn' (Lam. 1:4).

NN. "Had you had the merit, you would have read in the Torah: 'And you shall dwell in your land safely' (Lev. 26:5).

OO. "But since you did not have the merit: 'Judah has gone into exile because of affliction' (Lam. 1:3).

PP. "Had you had the merit, you would have read in the Torah: 'It was a night of watching unto the Lord' (Ex. 12:42).

QQ. "But since you did not have the merit: 'She weeps sore in the night' (Lam. 1:2).

RR. "Had you had the merit, you would have read in the Torah: 'How can I myself bear' (Dt. 1:12).

SS. "But since you did not have the merit: 'How lonely sits the city once great with people!' (Lam. 1:1)."

Dt. 28:47-8 makes precisely the point that the framer proposes to make. That is to say, if you had achieved the merit (using the theological language at hand), then you would have enjoyed everything, but since you did not have the merit, you enjoyed nothing. The sense of "merit" here clearly pertains to conditions of the covenant, that is, if you had attained merit through keeping the law.

The Rabbinic theology of covenant and grace encompasses all of humanity, Adam as much as Israel. Israel represents the counterpart to Adam. What happened to Adam in Eden happened to Israel in the Land. God mourned for Adam at the fall,

Seven. Knowing God: Lammentations Rabbah

and God mourned for Israel at the destruction. The same picture of God that Israel portrays humanity at large recognizes: the God who creates and commands, has high hopes for humanity but mourns its fall from grace:

LAMENTATIONS RABBAH IV.i.

1. A. R. Abbahu in the name of R. Yosé bar Haninah commenced [discourse by citing this verse]: "'But they are like a man, they have transgressed the covenant. There they dealt treacherously against me' (Hos. 6:7).
   B. "They are like a man, specifically, this refers to the first man [Adam]. [We shall now compare the story of the first man in Eden with the story of Israel in its land.]
   C. "Said the Holy One, blessed be He, 'In the case of the first man, I brought him into the garden of Eden, I commanded him, he violated my commandment, I judged him to be sent away and driven out, but I mourned for him, saying "How..." [which begins the book of Lamentations, hence stands for a lament, but which also is written with the consonants that also yield, Where are you].
   D. "'I brought him into the garden of Eden,' as it is written, And the Lord God took the man and put him into the garden of Eden (Gen. 2:15).
   E. "'I commanded him,' as it is written, And the Lord God commanded... (Gen. 2:16).
   F. "'And he violated my commandment,' as it is written, Did you eat from the tree concerning which I commanded you (Gen. 3:11).
   G. "'I judged him to be sent away,' as it is written, And the Lord God sent him from the garden of Eden (Gen. 3:23).
   H. "'And I judged him to be driven out.' And he drove out the man (Gen. 3:24).
   I. "'But I mourned for him, saying, How....' And He said to him, Where are you (Gen. 3:9), and the word for 'where are you' is written, How....
   J. "'So too in the case of his descendants, [God continues to speak,] I brought them into the Land of Israel, I commanded them, they violated my commandment, I judged them to be sent out and driven away but I mourned for them, saying, How....'
   K. "'I brought them into the Land of Israel:' 'And I brought you into the land of Carmel' (Jer. 2:7).
   L. "'I commanded them:' ' 'And you, command the children of Israel' (Ex. 27:20). 'command the children of Israel' (Lev. 24:2).
   M. "'They violated my commandment:' 'And all Israel have violated your Torah' (Dan. 9:11).
   N. "'I judged them to be sent out:' 'Send them away, out of my sight and let them go forth' (Jer. 15:1).
   O. "'....and driven away:' 'From my house I shall drive them' (Hos. 9:15).

P. "'But I mourned for them, saying, How...:' How lonely sits the city [that was full of people! How like a widow has she become, she that was great among the nations! She that was a princess among the cities has become a vassal. She weeps bitterly in the night, tears on her cheeks, among all her lovers she has none to comfort her; all her friends have dealt treacherously with her, they have become her enemies] (Lamentations 1:1-2)."

The evocation of the story of the first Man in the Garden of Eden to interpret the history of Israel in its Land produces a matching of details and a strong message, that after the disaster in Jeremiah's time, Israel fell from Eden – but could come back. God dwelt in the sanctuary but abandoned it before it was destroyed. Here the important detail registers: God mourned for the ruined Temple and left it only with sorrow. God wept. The imitation of God comes full circle. The Rabbinic theology imputes to God human emotions.

LAMENTATIONS RABBAH XXIV.II.

1. A. Another interpretation of the passage, "My Lord God of Hosts summoned on that day to weeping and lamenting, to tonsuring and girding with sackcloth:"
   B. When the Holy One, blessed be He, considered destroying the house of the sanctuary, he said, "So long as I am within it, the nations of the world cannot lay a hand on it.
   C. "I shall close my eyes to it and take an oath that I shall not become engaged with it until the time of the end."
   D. Then the enemies came and destroyed it.
   E. Forthwith the Holy One, blessed be He, took an oath by his right hand and put it behind him: "He has drawn back his right hand from before the enemy" (Lam. 2:3).
   F. At that moment the enemies entered the sanctuary and burned it up.
   G. When it had burned, the Holy One, blessed be He, said, "I do not have any dwelling on earth any more. I shall take up my presence from there and go up to my earlier dwelling."
   H. That is in line with this verse: "I will go and return to my place, until they acknowledge their guilt and seek my face" (Hos. 5:15).
   I. At that moment the Holy One, blessed be He, wept, saying, "Woe is me! What have I done! I have brought my Presence to dwell below on account of the Israelites, and now that they have sinned, I have gone back to my earlier dwelling. Heaven forfend that I now become a joke to the nations and a source of ridicule among people."
   J. At that moment Metatron came, prostrated himself, and said before him, "Lord of the world, let me weep, but don't you weep!"
   K. He said to him, "If you do not let me weep now, I shall retreat to a place in which you have no right to enter, and there I shall weep."

Seven. Knowing God: Lammentations Rabbah

L. That is in line with this verse: "But if you will not hear it, my soul shall weep in secret for pride" (Jer. 13:17).

2. **A. Said the Holy One, blessed be He, to the ministering angels, "Let's go and see what the enemies have done to my house."**

B. Forthwith the Holy One, blessed be He, and the ministering angels went forth, with Jeremiah before them.

C. When the Holy One, blessed be He, saw the house of the sanctuary, he said, "This is certainly my house, and this is my resting place, and the enemies have come and done whatever they pleased with it!"

D. At that moment the Holy One, blessed be He, wept, saying "Woe is me for my house! O children of mine – where are you? O priests of mine – where are you? O you who love me – where are you? What shall I do for you? I warned you, but you did not repent."

E. Said the Holy One, blessed be He, to Jeremiah, "Today I am like a man who had an only son, who made a marriage canopy for him, and the son died under his marriage canopy. Should you not feel pain for me and for my son?

F. "Go and call Abraham, Isaac, Jacob, and Moses from their graves, for they know how to weep."

G. He said before him, "Lord of the world, I don't know where Moses is buried."

H. The Holy One, blessed be He, said to him, "Go and stand at the bank of the Jordan and raise your voice and call him, 'Son of Amram, son of Amram, rise up and see your flock, which the enemy has swallowed up!'"

I. Jeremiah immediately went to the cave of Machpelah and said to the founders of the world, "Arise, for the time has come for you to be called before the Holy One, blessed be He."

J. They said to him, "Why?"

K. He said to them, "I don't know," because he was afraid that they would say to him, "In your time this has come upon our children!"

L. Jeremiah left them and went to the bank of the Jordan and cried out, "Son of Amram, son of Amram, rise up, for the time has come for you to be called before the Holy One, blessed be He."

M. He said to him, "What makes this day so special, that I am called before the Holy One, blessed be He?"

N. He said to them, "I don't know."

O. Moses left him and went to the ministering angels, for he had known them from the time of the giving of the Torah. He said to them, "You who serve on high! Do you know on what account I am summoned before the Holy One, blessed be He?"

P. They said to him, "Son of Amram! Don't you know that the house of the sanctuary has been destroyed, and the Israelites taken away into exile?"

Q. So he cried and wept until he came to the fathers of the world. They too forthwith tore their garments and put their hands on their heads, crying and weeping, up to the gates of the house of the sanctuary.

R. When the Holy One, blessed be He, saw them, forthwith: "My Lord God of Hosts summoned on that day to weeping and lamenting, to tonsuring and girding with sackcloth."

S. Were it not stated explicitly in a verse of Scripture, it would not be possible to make this statement.

T. And they went weeping from this gate to that, like a man whose deceased lies before him,

U. and the Holy One, blessed be He, wept, lamenting, "Woe for a king who prospers in his youth and not in his old age."

God's relationship with Israel transcends law and love and, just as the prophets had said, embodies divine pathos: God's engagement with suffering, sinning Israel. God's broken heart matching Israel's broken spirit.

II. TO WHOM, AND FOR WHOM, DOES THE DOCUMENT SPEAK? PROPOSITIONS AND PREOCCUPATIONS

The document speaks to an Israel that affirms God's unique relationship with Israel. That relationship works itself out even now, in a time of despair and disappointment. The resentment of the present condition, recapitulating the calamity of the destruction of the Temple in 586 and 70, finds its resolution and remission in the redemption that will follow Israel's regeneration through the Torah. But while the focus is as much on 70 as on 586, the Temple did not have to be destroyed a second time for the message to take shape. Nothing in the implicit norms of Lamentations Rabbah would have surprised the prophets of ancient Israelite times, reflecting on the Assyrian and Babylonian encounters. Rome merely followed suit. The preoccupation of Rabbinic Judaism represented here is that of the prophets, and the governing propositions restate in a new idiom the prophetic messages of the first Isaiah and of Jeremiah.

III. IMPLICIT TRUTHS

Lamentations Rabbah contains many articulated theological propositions, which form a set of claims as to truth. A survey of those claims shows that they systematize what is implicit in Scripture's narratives and form a coherent theological system out of those narratives. A brief survey of the particular propositions expressed in the document yields a massive rehearsal in detail of a few basic convictions. I provide a brief epitome of the main points that register, identifying the passages in which they occur in sequence.

Israel's relationship with God is treated with special reference to the covenant, the Torah, and the land. By reason of the sins of the Israelites, they have gone into exile with the destruction of the Temple. The founders of the family, Abraham, Isaac, and Jacob, also went into exile. Now they cannot be accused of lacking in religious duties, attention to teachings of the Torah and of prophecy, carrying out the requirements of righteousness (philanthropy) and good deeds, and the like. The people are at fault for their own condition (I:i.1-7). Torah-study defines the condition of Israel, e.g., "If you have seen [the inhabitants of] towns uprooted from their places in the land of Israel, know that it is because they did not pay the salary of scribes and teachers" (II.i).

So long as Judah and Benjamin — meaning, in this context, the surviving people, after the northern tribes were taken away by the Assyrians — were at home, God could take comfort at the loss of the ten tribes; once they went into exile, God began to mourn (II:ii). Israel (now meaning not the northern tribes, but the remaining Jews) survived Pharaoh and Sennacherib, but not God's punishment (III:i). After the disaster in Jeremiah's time, Israel emerged from Eden — but could come back. (IV:i). God did not play favorites among the tribes; when any of them sinned, he punished them through exile (VI:i). Israel was punished because of the ravaging of words of Torah and prophecy, righteous men, religious duties and good deeds (VII:i). The land of Israel, the Torah, and the Temple are ravaged, to the shame of Israel (Jer. 9:19-21) (VIII:i). The Israelites practiced idolatry, still more did the pagans; God was neglected by the people and was left solitary, so God responded to the people's actions (X:i). If you had achieved the merit (using the theological language at hand), then you would have enjoyed everything, but since you did not have the merit, you enjoyed nothing (XI:i).

The Israelites (throughout referring to the surviving Jews, after the northern tribes were taken into exile) did not trust God, so they suffered disaster ((XIII.i). The Israelites scorned God and brought dishonor upon God among the nations (XV:i). While God was generous with the Israelites in the wilderness, under severe conditions, he was harsh with them in civilization, under pleasant conditions, because they sinned and angered him (XVI:i). With merit one drinks good water in Jerusalem, without, bad water in the exile of Babylonia; with merit one sings songs and Psalms in Jerusalem, without, dirges and lamentations in Babylonia. At stake is peoples' merit, not God's grace (XIX:i). The contrast is drawn between redemption and disaster, the giving of the Torah and the destruction of the Temple (XX:i). When the Israelites went into exile among the nations of the world, not one of them could produce a word of Torah from his mouth; God punished Israel for its sins (XXI:i). Idolatry was the cause (XXII:i). The destruction of the Temple was possible only because God had already abandoned it (XXIV:ii). When the Temple was destroyed, God was answerable to the patriarchs for what he had done (XXIV:ii). The Presence of God departed from the Temple by stages (XXV:i).

The Holy One punishes Israel only after bringing testimony against them (XXVII:i). The road that led from the salvation of Hezekiah is the one that brought Israel to the disaster brought about by Nebuchadnezzar. Then the Israelite kings believed, but the pagan king did not believe; and God gave the Israelite kings a reward for their faith, through Hezekiah, and to the pagan king, without his believing and without obeying, were handed over Jerusalem and its Temple (XXX:i). Before the Israelites went into exile, the Holy One, blessed be he, called them bad. But when they had gone into exile, he began to sing their praises (XXXI:i). The Israelites were sent into exile only after they had defied the Unique One of the world, the Ten Commandments, circumcision, which had been given to the twentieth generation (=Abraham), and the Pentateuch (XXXV:ii, iii). When the Temple was destroyed and Israel went into exile, God mourned in the manner that mortals do (XXXV:iv). The prophetic critique of Israel is mitigated by mercy. Israel stands in an ambiguous relationship with God, both divorced and not divorced (XXXV:vi, vii).

Before God penalizes, he has already prepared the healing for the penalty. As to all the harsh prophecies that Jeremiah issued against the Israelites, Isaiah first of all anticipated each and pronounced healing for it (XXXVI:ii). The Israelites err for weeping frivolously, "but in the end there will be a real weeping for good cause" (XXXVI:iv, v). The ten tribes went into exile, but the Presence of God did not go into exile. Judah and Benjamin went into exile, but the Presence of God did not go into exile. But when the children went into exile, then the Presence of God went into exile (XXXIX:iii). The great men of Israel turned their faces away when they saw people sinning, and God did the same to them (XL:ii). When the Israelites carry out the will of the Holy One, they add strength to the strength of heaven, and when they do not, they weaken the power of the One above (XL:ii). The exile and the redemption will match (XL:ii). In her affliction, Jerusalem remembered her rebellion against God (XLI;i).

When the gentile nations sin, there is no sequel in punishment, but when the Israelites sin, they also are punished (XLII:i). God considered carefully how to bring the evil upon Israel (XLVIII:i). God suffers with Israel and for Israel (L:i), a minor theme in a massive compilation of stories. By observing their religious duties the Israelites became distinguished before God (LIII:i). With every thing with which the Israelites sinned, they were smitten, and with that same thing they will be comforted. When they sinned with the head, they were smitten at the head, but they were comforted through the head (LVI:i). There is an exact match between Israel's triumph and Israel's downfall. Thus: Just as these — the people of Jericho — were punished through the destruction effected by priest and prophet [the priests and Joshua at Jericho], so these — the people of Jerusalem in the time of the Babylonian conquest — were subject to priest and prophet [Jeremiah]. Just as these who were punished were penalized through the ram's horn and shouting, so Israel will be saved through ram's horn and shouting (LVII:ii).

God's relationship to Israel was complicated by the relationship to Jacob, thus: "Isn't it the fact that the Israelites are angering me only because of the icon of Jacob that is engraved on my throne? Here, take it, it's thrown in your face!" (LVII:ii). God is engaged with Israel's disaster (LIX:ii). The Israelites did not fully explore

Seven. Knowing God: Lammentations Rabbah

the limits of the measure of justice, so the measure of justice did not go to extremes against them (LX:i, LXI:i). God's decree against Jerusalem comes from of old (LXIV:i). God forewarned Israel and showed Israel favor, but it did no good (LXIX:i). God did to Israel precisely what he had threatened long ago (LXXIII:i). But God does not rejoice in punishing Israel. The argument between God and Israel is framed in this way. The Community of Israel says that they are the only ones who accepted God; God says, I rejected everybody else for you (LXXIX:ii). Israel accepted its suffering as atonement and asked that the suffering expiate the sin (LXXV:i).

God suffers along with Israel, Israel's loyalty will be recognized and appreciated by God, and, in the meantime, the Israelites will find in the Torah the comfort that they require. The nations will be repaid for their actions toward Israel in the interval. Even though the Holy One, blessed be he, is angry with his servants, the righteous, in this world, in the world to come he goes and has mercy on them (LXXXVI:i). God is good to those that deserve it (LXXXVII:i). God mourns for Israel the way human mourners mourn (LXXXVIII:i). God will never abandon Israel (LXXXIX:i). The Holy Spirit brings about redemption (XCV:i). It is better to be punished by God than favored by a gentile king, thus: "Better was the removing of the ring by Pharaoh [for the sealing of decrees to oppress the Israelites] than the forty years during which Moses prophesied concerning them, because it was through this [oppression] that the redemption came about, while through that [prophesying] the redemption did not come about" (CXXII:i).

The upshot here is that persecution in the end is good for Israel, because it produces repentance more rapidly than prophecy ever did, with the result that the redemption is that much nearer. The enemy will also be punished for its sins, and, further, God's punishment is appropriate and well-placed. People get what they deserve, both Israel and the others. God should protect Israel and not leave them among the nations, but that is not what he has done (CXXIII:i). God blames that generation for its own fate, and the ancestors claim that the only reason the Israelites endure is because of the merit of the ancestors. (CXXIX:i). The redemption of the past tells us about the redemption in the future (CXXX:i). "The earlier generations, because they smelled the stench of only part of the tribulations inflicted by the idolatrous kingdoms, became impatient. But we, who dwell in the midst of the four kingdoms, how much the more [are we impatient]!" (CXXXI:i).

God's redemption is certain, so people who are suffering should be glad, since that is a guarantee of coming redemption; thus "For if those who outrage him he treats in such a way, those who do his will all the more so!" So if the words of the prophet Uriah are carried out, the words of the prophet Zechariah will be carried out, while if the words of the prophet Uriah prove false, then the words of the prophet Zechariah will not be true either. "I was laughing with pleasure because the words of Uriah have been carried out, and that means that the words of Zechariah in the future will be carried out" (CXL:i). The Temple will be restored, and Israel will regain its place, as God's throne and consort, respectively]. (CXLI:i). Punishment and rejection will be followed by forgiveness and reconciliation (CXLII:i). The Jews can accomplish part of the task on their own, even though they throw themselves wholly on God's mercy. The desired age is either like that of Adam, or like that of Moses and Solomon, or like that of Noah and Abel; all three possibilities link the coming redemption to a time of perfection, Eden, or the age prior to idolatry, or the time of Moses and Solomon, the builders of the Tabernacle and the Temple, respectively (CXLIII:i). If there is rejection, then there is no hope, but if there is anger, there is hope, because someone who is angry may in the end be appeased. Whenever there is an allusion to divine anger, that too is a mark of hope (CXLIV:i).

Israel's relationship with the nations is treated with interest in Israel's history, past, present, and future, and how that pattern is to be known. But there is no theory of "the other," or the outsider here; the nations are the enemy; the compilers find nothing of merit to report about them. Israel's difference from the other, for which God is responsible, accounts for the dislike that the nations express toward Israel; Israel's present condition as minority, different and despised on account of the difference, is God's fault and choice. Israel was besieged not only by the Babylonians but also the neighbors, the Ammonites and Moabites (IX:i), and God will punish them too. The public ridicule of Jews' religious rites contrasts with the Jews' own perception of their condition. The exposition of Ps. 69:13 in terms of gentiles' ridicule of Jews' practices — the Jews' poverty, their Sabbath and Seventh Year observance, — is followed by a re-exposition of the Jews' practices, now with respect to the ninth of Ab (XVII:i). Even though the nations of the world go into exile, their exile is not really an exile at all. But as for Israel, their exile really is an exile. The nations of the world, who eat the bread and drink the wine of others, do not really experience exile. But the Israelites, who do not eat the bread and drink the wine of others, really do experience exile (XXXVII:i).

The Ammonites and Moabites joined with the enemy and behaved very spitefully (XLIV:i). When the Israelites fled from the destruction of Jerusalem, the nations of the world sent word everywhere to which they fled and shut them out (LV:i). But this was to be blamed on God: "If we had intermarried with them, they would have accepted us." LXIX:i There are ten references to "might" of Israel; when the Israelites sinned, these forms of might were taken away from them and given to the nations of the world. The nations of the world ridicule the Jews for their religious observances (LXXXIII:i). These propositions simply expose, in their own framework, the same proposition as the ones concerning God's relationship to Israel and Israel's relationship to God. The relationship between Israel and the nations forms a subset of the relationship of Israel and God; nothing in the former relationship happens on its own, but all things express in this mundane context the rules and effects of the rules that govern in the transcendent one. All we learn about Israel and the nations is that the covenant endures, bearing its own inevitable sanctions and consequences.

Seven. Knowing God: Lammentations Rabbah

Our authorship has little interest in Israel out of relationship with either God or the nations. Israel on its own forms a subordinated and trivial theme; whatever messages we do find take on meaning only in the initial framework, that defined by Israel's relationship with God. Israel is never on its own. The bitterness of the ninth of Ab is contrasted with the bitter herbs with which the first redemption is celebrated (XVIII:i). The same contrast is drawn between the giving of the Torah and the destruction of the Temple (XX:i). If Israel had found rest among the nations, she would not have returned to the holy land (XXXVII:ii). The glory of Israel lay in its relationship to God, in the sanhedrin, in the disciples of sages, in the priestly watches, in the children (XL:i). Israel first suffers, then rejoices; her unfortunate condition marks the fact that Israel stands at the center of things (LIX:iii). Israel has declined through the generations, thus: "In olden times, when people held the sanhedrin in awe, naughty words were never included in songs. But when the sanhedrin was abolished, naughty words were inserted in songs. In olden times, when troubles came upon Israel, they stopped rejoicing on that account. Now that both have come to an end [no more singing, no more banquet halls], 'The joy of our hearts has ceased; our dancing has been turned to mourning.'" (CXXXVII:i).

It would be difficult to construct a more authoritative epitome of Scripture's picture of Israelite history and salvation than this detailed commentary on Lamentations. Yet what emerges is a picture of God that expresses what is distinctive to that Judaic response to Scripture: God who weeps, God who suffers with Israel, for Israel. All of nature participates in the creator's mourning. That is what Israel knows about God in the norm of Lamentations Rabbah: nature and Israel correspond in relationship to God:

LAMENTATIONS RABBAH XXXV:IV.

1. A. Another matter concerning "[How] lonely sits [the city that was full of people]" [now with stress on "sits," in its sense of "sitting in mourning:"]
   B. Said R. Nahman said Samuel in the name of R. Joshua b. Levi, "The Holy One, blessed be He, asked the ministering angels, 'A mortal king in mourning – what is fitting for him to do?'
   C. "They said to him, 'He hangs sacking on his door.'
   D. "He said to them, 'I too will do so:' 'I clothe the heavens with blackness, and I make sackcloth their covering' (Isa. 50:3).
   E. "'What else does a mortal king do?'
   F. "'He turns down the lamps.'
   G. "'I too will do so:' 'The sun and the moon are become black, the stars withdraw their shining' (Joel 4:15).
   H. "'What else?'
   I. "'He turns over the couch.'
   J. "'I too:' 'Until thrones were cast down, and One that was ancient of days did sit' (Dan. 7:9).
   K. "It is as though they were overturned [in mourning].

L. "'What else?'
M. "'He goes barefoot.'
N. "'I too:' 'The Lord in the whirlwind and in the storm is his way, and clouds are the dust of his feet' (Nah. 1:5).
O. "'What else?'
P. "'He tears his purple clothing.'
Q. "'I too:' 'The Lord has done that which he devised, he has performed his word' (Lam. 2:17)."
T. [Continuing from Q:] "'What else?'
U. "'He sits in silence.'
V. "'I too:' 'He sits alone and keeps silent' (Lam. 3:28).
W. "'What else?'
X. "'He sits and weeps.'
Y. "'I too: "How lonely sits the city that was full of people."'"

The implicit norm then is, nature corresponds to his body. We shall now see that Israel his soul-mate.

8

Loving, and Being Loved by, God: Song of Songs Rabbah

I. THE DOCUMENT AND ITS PROGRAM: RECURRENT QUESTIONS

Norms govern beyond the measure of the law with its programs of actions of omission and commission. Beyond the measure of the law, norms define right attitudes and aspirations. The final implicit norm in this canonical survey imposes the obligation to love, and be loved by, God: that variable of sentiment and emotion that the law cannot in the end require but to which, in the Torah, God aspires: "You will love the Lord your God with all your heart, with all your soul, and with all your might." That norm is implicit throughout and explicitly set forth in Song of Songs Rabbah, a commentary on the Song of Songs (a,k.a., Song of Solomon).

The Song of Songs finds a place in the Torah because that collection of love-songs in fact speaks about the relationship between God and Israel. The intent of the compilers of Song of Songs Rabbah, a document of indeterminate date and venue, is to justify that reading. What this means is that Midrash-exegesis turns to everyday experience — the love of husband and wife — for a metaphor of God's love for Israel and Israel's love for God. Then, when Solomon's song says, "O that you would kiss me with the kisses of your mouth! For your love is better than wine," (Song 1:2), the sages think of how God kissed Israel — leaning down at Sinai, for example. Reading the Song of Songs as a metaphor, the Judaic sages state in a systematic and orderly way the implicit norms that are realized in the explicit teachings and practices of the Torah. The sages' power, through repetition and implicit disapproval of what they do not celebrate, to define dogma and designate heresy forms the point of interest of that document for this study.

If the principal parts of the Rabbinic system — stress on Torah-learning, divine justice and mercy, reward and punishment after death, and the election of Israel, for example — formed the implicit doctrines of tractate Abot, then the articulation of the system whole and in complete detail would define the contribution of Song of Songs Rabbah. The implicit theology of that document fully exposes the system as a whole, taking a position on the important questions facing any construction built on the foundation of Scripture. To put matters simply: one composition after another in Song of Songs Rabbah states a fully exposed, and complete account of the way of life and the world view of Rabbinic Judaism, embodied in detail. If, accordingly, we wish to define Judaism, its way of life and world view as a coherent system, we need only turn to the compositions of Song of Songs Rabbah that do just that.

Before showing the way in which the message of the system as a whole comes to expression in this remarkable document, let me give a single example of the systematic exposition of theology, with stress on the Halakhic medium of that theology. As is its way, Song of Songs Rabbah forms a long list of examples, in Judaic norms of conduct, for the beauty imputed to Israel by the exegetes of Song of Songs Rabbah within their encompassing theory that the Song portrays Israel as the beloved, God as the lover, of the poetry:

SONG OF SONGS RABBAH XCV:I

1. A. "Behold, you are beautiful, my love; behold, you are beautiful" (Song 7:6):
   B. "Behold you are beautiful" in religious deeds,
   C. "Behold you are beautiful" in acts of grace,
   D. "Behold you are beautiful" in carrying out religious obligations of commission,
   E. "Behold you are beautiful" in carrying out religious obligations of omission,
   F. "Behold you are beautiful" in carrying out the religious duties of the home, in separating priestly ration and tithes,
   G. "Behold you are beautiful" in carrying out the religious duties of the field, gleanings, forgotten sheaves, the corner of the field, poor person's tithe, and declaring the field ownerless.
   H. "Behold you are beautiful" in observing the taboo against mixed species.
   I. "Behold you are beautiful" in providing a linen cloak with woolen show-fringes.
   J. "Behold you are beautiful" in [keeping the rules governing] planting,
   K. "Behold you are beautiful" in keeping the taboo on uncircumcised produce,
   L. "Behold you are beautiful" in keeping the laws on produce in the fourth year after the planting of an orchard,
   M. "Behold you are beautiful" in circumcision,
   N. "Behold you are beautiful" in trimming the wound,
   O. "Behold you are beautiful" in reciting the Prayer,
   P. *"Behold you are beautiful" in reciting the* Shema,
   Q. *"Behold you are beautiful" in putting a* mezuzah *on the doorpost of your house,*

Eight. Loving and Being Loved by, God: Song of Songs Rabbah

R. "Behold you are beautiful" in wearing phylacteries,
S. "Behold you are beautiful" in building the tabernacle for the Festival of Tabernacles,
T. "Behold you are beautiful" in taking the palm branch and etrog on the Festival of Tabernacles,
U. "Behold you are beautiful" in repentance,
V. "Behold you are beautiful" in good deeds,
W. "Behold you are beautiful" in this world,
X. "Behold you are beautiful" in the world to come.

The exposition of the cited verse identifies traits of beauty in Israel and finds them in Israel's realization of the commandments. The catalogue begins with encompassing categories, religious deeds and actions beyond the measure of the law; then religious obligations of commission and of omission. Then come laws of agriculture, F-L; circumcision, M-N; liturgical obligations, O-P, and a mixture of ritual and moral commandments, the mezuzah called for by the Shema and the phylacteries donned in the morning recitation of the Shema, the Festival, S-T, the moral virtues of repentance and the doing of good deeds, this world and the next world.

The miscellaneous character of the particular items should not obscure the implicit propositions in play. First, God and Israel are the speakers of Song of Songs. Second, Israel's obedience to the laws of the Torah represent acts of love, realizations of Israel's devotion to God and eagerness to do as he commands. Then comes a mixture of commandments, concerning the community at large (agricultural taboos), actions of the individual (liturgical obligations), examples of seasonal obligations (tabernacle), embodiments of moral virtue, repentance, good deeds, with the climax at the end: the attainment of beauty in this world and in the world to come: resurrection and life eternal.

Exemplary lists of the several classes of virtuous conduct and conviction, public and personal, involving action and attitude, characterize Song of Songs Rabbah, which attests to the complete and definitive definition of Rabbinic Judaism, not only in principle but in practice. No such systematic statements effected through list-making predominates in documents that came to closure in the earlier phases of the Rabbinic canon. And the orthodoxy permeated by love and grace expressed here completed the doctrinal exposition begun, in generalities, in tractate Abot. What commences there in generalizations concludes here in particularizations. What imparts to the whole urgency is the simple fact that other Judaic systems — that is, religious systems built on the Scriptures held in common by them all — take up other positions on the religious imperatives of the Torah, the nature of God revealed by the Torah, and life after death, to take three among many controverted matters. Indeed, That is made explicit:

Mishnah-tractate Sanhedrin 10:1
C. And these are the ones who have no portion in the world to come:
D. He who says, the resurrection of the dead is a teaching which does not derive from the Torah, and the Torah does not come from Heaven; and an Epicurean.

Denial of the dogma of resurrection of the dead and of the Torah's sponsorship of that dogma represents a cause for the extreme penalty of extinction through all eternity. Then "in this world, in the world to come" signals that at issue is a matter of debate among Judaisms. We have then to consider that the entire program of norms of conviction and conduct that infuses the poem represents an explicit position on matters of debate. It follows that in the Rabbinic system implicit norms respond to contrary ones held by other circles governed, start to finish. The protracted catalogues of virtues of deed and deliberation, action and attitude, have to be read as party platforms, judgments on matters of debate among Israelites in the several communities of Judaism. For the later centuries of late antiquity we do not have any direct knowledge of other communities of Judaism besides the one represented by the Rabbinic canon. We have only the Rabbinic sages' words to signal the character of their opposition: what they stress, what they do not acknowledge. But those words bear unmistakable signals of the activity of a program of orthodoxy and exclusion: these beliefs belie contrary ones, which in the present case are made articulate.

This brief survey of Song of Songs Rabbah completes the demonstration of the presence of a normative theology of Rabbinic Judaism at its fundamental level. Israel loves and is loved by God, and that love, fulfilling and transcending the covenant, comes to expression in Israel's realization of the Torah and God's response to Israel's love embodied by religious duties: responses to the commandments of God. Gnostics and various Christianities present candidates for those that take contrary positions on a shared agendum. The Rabbinic sages repeat themselves in diverse ways and contexts, time and again to stress their position on a public debate. It was not ordinarily their way to identify those whom they opposed. Their points of emphasis permit us to construct that opposition and to identify it. In the survey of their expositions of their system, addressed in the discussion of implicit truths, part iii below, we confront the account of orthodoxy that defines, willy-nilly, the character of heresy.

II. TO WHOM, AND FOR WHOM, DOES THE DOCUMENT SPEAK? PROPOSITIONS AND PREOCCUPATIONS

The document speaks to a world of Judaisms, one that was filled with competition, and for a completed system of thought. It takes for granted a fully exposed program of conduct as well. The emphasis on Torah-learning marks the document as quintessentially Rabbinic: it speaks for Rabbis about their

Eight. Loving and Being Loved by, God: Song of Songs Rabbah

preoccupations. The document moreover joins imperatives of action and attitude, typical of Rabbinic Judaism. Every Rabbinic document states the priority of Torah-learning and Song of Songs Rabbah conforms. But in its list-making approach, illustrated in what follows, it finds a larger context in which Torah-learning is located. Specifically, it joins Torah-study with a list of those prepared to give their lives for the Torah, Abraham, Isaac, Moses, Elijah, Hananiah, Mishael, and Azariah. Then come well-founded laws and lore, Halakhah and Aggadah. All this leads to the preoccupation of the document, the basic doctrine of the Rabbinic system, continuing prophecy: Israel's condition responds to Israel's conviction and conduct: everything wrong with Israel, and everything right, derive from the Torah, which is why Israel is beloved of God. Here in a nutshell is the entirety of the Rabbinic system:

Song of Songs Rabbah XXII:i
1. A. "Sustain me with raisins, refresh me with apples; for I am sick with love (Song 2:5):"
   B. [With reference to letters of the word for raisins, we interpret the opening clause:] with two fires, the fire above, the fire below [the heavenly fire, the altar fire].
2. A. Another explanation: "Sustain me with raisins:"
   B. with two fires, the Torah in Writing, the Torah in Memory.
3. A. Another explanation: "Sustain me with raisins:"
   B. with many fires, the fire of Abraham, the fire of Moriah, the fire of the bush, the fire of Elijah, and the fire of Hananiah, Mishael, and Azariah.
4. A. Another explanation: "Sustain me with raisins:"
   B. This refers to the well-founded laws.
5. A. "...refresh me with apples:"
   B. this refers to the lore, the fragrance and taste of which are like apples.
6. A. "...for I am sick with love:"
   B. Said the Congregation of Israel before the Holy One, blessed be He, "Lord of the world, all of the illnesses that you bring upon me are so as to make me more beloved to you."
7. A. Another interpretation of the phrase, "for I am sick with love:"
   B. Said the Congregation of Israel before the Holy One, blessed be He, "Lord of the world, all of the illnesses that you bring upon me are because I love you."
8. A. Another interpretation of the phrase, "for I am sick with love:]"
   B. "Even though I am sick, I am beloved unto him."

In reading the love-songs of the Song of Songs as the story of the love affair of God and Israel, sages identify implicit meanings that are always few and invariably self-evident; no serious effort goes into demonstrating the fact that God speaks, or Israel speaks; the point of departure is the message and meaning the One or the other means to convey. To take one instance, time and again we shall be told that a certain expression of love in the poetry of the Song of Songs is God's speaking to Israel about [1] the Sea, [2] Sinai, and [3] the world to come; or [1] the first redemption, the one from Egypt; [2] the second redemption, the one from Babylonia; and [3] the third redemption, the one at the end of days. The repertoire of symbols covers Temple and schoolhouse, personal piety and public worship, and other matched pairs and sequences of coherent matters, all of them seen as embedded within the poetry. Here is Scripture's poetry read as metaphor, and the task of the reader is well-balanced that for which each image of the poem stands.

So Israel's holy life is metaphorized through the poetry of love and beloved, Lover and Israel. Long lists of alternative meanings or interpretations end up saying just one thing, but in different ways. The implicit meanings prove very few indeed. When in Song of Songs Rabbah we have a sequence of items alleged to form a taxon, that is, a set of things that share a common indicative quality, what we have is a list. The list presents diverse matters that all together share, and therefore also set forth, a single fact or rule or phenomenon. That is why we can list them, in all their distinctive character and specificity, in a common catalogue of "other things" that pertain all together to one thing. So much for the propositions and preoccupations of the document. Now we turn to its implicit truths, the generative dogmas that define the community of Judaism that has produced and preserved this document within its canon.

III. IMPLICIT TRUTHS

In reading the love-songs of the Song of Songs as the story of the love affair of God and Israel, sages identify implicit meanings that are always few and invariably self-evident; no serious effort goes into demonstrating the fact that God speaks, or Israel speaks; the point of departure is the message and meaning the One or the other means to convey.

To take one instance, time and again we shall be told that a certain expression of love in the poetry of the Song of Songs is God's speaking to Israel about [1] the Sea, [2] Sinai, and [3] the world to come; or [1] the first redemption, the one from Egypt; [2] the second redemption, the one from Babylonia; and [3] the third redemption, the one at the end of days. The repertoire of symbols covers Temple and schoolhouse, personal piety and public worship, and other matched pairs and sequences of coherent matters, all of them seen as embedded within the poetry. Here is Scripture's poetry read as metaphor, and the task of the reader is well-balanced that for which each image of the poem stands. So Israel's holy life is metaphorized through the poetry of love and beloved, Lover and Israel. Long lists of alternative meanings or interpretations end up saying just one thing, but in different ways. The implicit meanings prove very few indeed. When in Song of Songs Rabbah we have a sequence of items alleged to form a taxon, that is, a set of things that share a common taxic indicator, what we have is a list. The list presents diverse

Eight. Loving and Being Loved by, God: Song of Songs Rabbah

matters that all together share, and therefore also set forth, a single fact or rule or phenomenon. That is why we can list them, in all their distinctive character and specificity, in a common catalogue of "other things" that pertain all together to one thing.

What do the compilers say through their readings of the metaphor of — to take one interesting example — the nut-tree for Israel? And with whom do they contend?

Song of Songs Rabbah LXXXVII:i

1. A. Another explanation of the phrase, "I went down to the nut orchard (Song 6:11):"
   B. Said R. Joshua b. Levi, "The Israelites are compared to a nut tree:
   C. "just as a nut tree is pruned and improved thereby, for, like hair that is trimmed and grows more abundantly, and like nails that are trimmed and grow more abundantly,
   D. "so is the case with Israel, for they are pruned of the return on their work, which they gave to those who labor in the Torah in this world, and it is for their good that they are so pruned, for that increases their wealth in this world and the reward that is coming to them in the world to come."

4. A. [Supply: "the nut orchard:"]
   B. R. Azariah made two statements:
   C. "Just as in the case of a nut, the husk guards the fruit, so the unlettered people in Israel strengthen [those who are engaged in] study of the Torah: 'It is a tree of life to those who strengthen her' (Prov. 83:18)."
   D. He made another statement: "Just as if a nut falls into the mud, you take it and wipe it and rinse it and wash it and it is perfectly fine for eating, so in the case of Israel, however they are made filthy in transgressions throughout the days of the year, the Day of Atonement comes along and covers over their sins: 'For on this day shall atonement be made for you, to cleanse you' (Lev. 16:30)."

5. A. [Supply: "the nut orchard:"]
   B. R. Judah b. R. Simon says, "Just as a nut has two shells, so the Israelites have two religious duties, the act of circumcision and the act of cutting away the flesh of the penis."

6. A. Another explanation of the phrase, "I went down to the nut orchard:"
   B. Said R. Simeon b. Laqish, "Just as a nut tree is unwrinkled,
   D. "so whoever climbs to the top of it and does not pay attention to how he is climbing will fall down and die and get his from the nut tree,
   E. "so whoever exercises authority over the community in Israel and does not pay a mind to how he governs Israel in the end will fall and get his on their account:

F. "'Israel is the Lord's holy portion, his first fruits of the increase, all who consume him will be held guilty' (Jer. 2:3)."
7. A. Another explanation of the phrase, "I went down to the nut orchard:"
B. Just as a nut is a toy for children and a treat for kings,
C. so are the Israelites in this world on account of transgression: "I am become a joke to all my people" (Lam. 3:14),
D. but in the world to come: "kings will be your foster fathers" (Isa. 49:23).
8. A. Another explanation of the phrase, "I went down to the nut orchard:"
B. Just as in the case of a nut tree, there are soft ones, medium ones, and hard ones,
C. so in the case of Israel, there are those who carry out acts of righteousness [through charity] on their own volition, there are those whom you ask and will give, and there are those whom you ask and who do nothing.
9. A. Another explanation of the phrase, "I went down to the nut orchard:"
B. just as in the case of a nut, a stone breaks it,
C. so the Torah is called a stone, [and] the impulse to do evil is called a stone.
D. The Torah is called a stone: "And I will give you the tablets of stone" (Ex. 24:12).
E. The impulse to do evil is called a stone: "And I will take away the stony heart out of your flesh" (Ezek. 36:26).
10. A. Another explanation of the phrase, "I went down to the nut orchard:"
B. Just as a stone cannot deceive the customs collector because it is betrayed by its rattle,
C. So with the Israelites, in any place to which one of them goes, he cannot say, "I'm not a Jew."
D. Why not?
E. Because he is a marked man: "All who see them will recognize them, that they are the seed which the Lord has blessed" (Isa. 61:9).
11. A. Another explanation of the phrase, "I went down to the nut orchard:"
B. Just as in the case of a nut, if you have a full bag of nuts in hand, you can still put in any amount of sesame seeds and mustard seeds and there will be room for them,
C. so how many proselytes have come and been attached to Israel: "Who has counted the dust of Jacob" (Num. 23:10).
12. A. Another explanation of the phrase, "I went down to the nut orchard:"
B. Just as in the case of a nut, if you take one out of the pile, all the rest fall down on one another,
C. so in the case of Israel, if one of them is smitten, all of them feel it:

Eight. Loving and Being Loved by, God: Song of Songs Rabbah

    D. "Shall one man sin and you will be angry with all the congregation" (Num. 16:22).
14. A. Another explanation: "I went down to the nut orchard:"
    B. This is the world.
    C. "to look at the blossoms of the valley:"
    D. This is Israel.
    E. "to see whether the vines had budded:" this refers to synagogues and houses of study.
    F. "whether the pomegranates were in bloom:"
    G. This refers to children who are in session, occupied with the Torah, sitting row by row like pomegranate seeds."

Let us first identify the polemic. LXXXVII:i.1 defends the use of scarce resources for the support of Torah-sages. This brings a reward in the world to come and so is worthwhile. Critics of the Rabbis for pruning the return on the labor of ordinary folk in favor of support for the Rabbis have their answer. No. 4 says the same thing: the unlettered people in Israel strengthen those who study the Torah. No. 5 proceeds to the matter of circumcision, we know an issue between Judaic and Christian debaters. No. 6 reverts to those that govern Israel. Now the government is subject to criticism, the government that pays no heed to how it governs Israel. The Rabbinic struggle with the patriarchate in the Land of Israel and the exilarchate in Babylonia comes to mind. Israel's fate in this world does ot complete the story, No. 7; Israel suffers now but will find its reward. No. 8 forms a social commentary n the motivation of those that give: of their own volition, when asked, and so on. The Torah breaks the impulse to do evil. The Israelite cannot deny his identity. There is plenty of room in Israel for proselytes, No. 11. All Israel suffers the fate of each Israelite, No. 12. No. 14 reverts to where we started.

What are the implicit doctrines on which the poet-exegetes draw? First, Israel gains from sacrifice in favor of Torah-study. Israel prospers when it gives scarce resources for the study of the Torah or for carrying out religious duties; second, Israel sins but atones, and Torah is the medium of atonement; third, Israel is identified through carrying out its religious duties, e.g., circumcision; fourth, Israel's leaders had best watch their step; fifth, Israel may be nothing well-balanced but will be in glory in the coming age; sixth, Israel has plenty of room for outsiders but cannot afford to lose a single member. What we have is a repertoire of fundamentals, dealing with Torah and Torah-study, the moral life and atonement, Israel and its holy way of life, Israel and its coming salvation. Those that fall outside of the Rabbinic circles form the obvious target of the polemic encased in the exegesis of the cited verse.

What of God and Israel? Here the exegetes explain how God has loved Israel but has punished her for her iniquities, love and jealousy forming the poles of the relationship:

Song of Songs Rabbah CVIII:II

1. A. "for love is strong as death:"
   B. As strong as death is the love with which the Holy One, blessed be He, loves Israel: "I have loved you says the Lord" (Mal. 1:2).
   C. "jealousy is cruel as the grave:"
   D. That is when they make him jealous with their idolatry: "They roused him to jealousy with strange gods" (Dt. 32:16).
2. A. Another explanation of "for love is strong as death:"
   B. As strong as death is the love with which Isaac loved Esau: "Now Isaac loved Esau" (Gen. 25:28).
   C. "jealousy is cruel as the grave:"
   D. The jealousy that Esau held against Jacob: "And Esau hated Jacob" (Gen. 27:41).
3. A. Another explanation of "for love is strong as death:"
   B. As strong as death is the love with which Jacob loved Joseph: "Now Israel loved Joseph more than all his children" (Gen. 37:3).
   C. "jealousy is cruel as the grave:"
   D. The jealousy that his brothers held against him: "And his brothers envied him" (Gen. 37:11).
4. A. Another explanation of "for love is strong as death:"
   B. As strong as death is the love with which Jonathan loved David: "And Jonathan loved him as his own soul" (1 Sam. 18:1).
   C. "jealousy is cruel as the grave:"
   D. The jealousy of Saul against David: "And Saul eyed David" (1 Sam. 18:9).
5. A. Another explanation of "for love is strong as death:"
   B. As strong as death is the love with which a man loves his wife: "Enjoy life with the wife whom you love" (Qoh. 9:9).
   C. "jealousy is cruel as the grave:"
   D. The jealousy that she causes in him and leads him to say to her, "Do not speak with such-and-so."
   E. If she goes and speaks with that man, forthwith: "The spirit of jealousy comes upon him and he is jealous on account of his wife" (Num. 5:14).
6. A. Another explanation of "for love is strong as death:"
   B. As strong as death is the love with which the generation that suffered the repression loved the Holy One, blessed be He: "No, but for your sake we are killed all day long" (Ps. 44:23).
   C. "jealousy is cruel as the grave:"
   D. The jealousy that the Holy One, blessed be He, will hold for Zion, that is a great zealousness: "Thus says the Lord, I am jealous for Zion with a great jealousy" (Zech. 1:14).

We begin with a general pattern: God's love for Israel is as strong as death, his jealousy is as cruel as the grave, so idolatry stands for death, God's love for life. God's love is like the love of Isaac for Israel, his jealousy is like the jealous of Esau for Jacob, Jonathan's love for David, Saul's jealousy of Davis; so too

Eight. Loving and Being Loved by, God: Song of Songs Rabbah

Jacob's love for Joseph, Joseph's brothers jealousy. We end with the climax with its jarring shift in the context of jealousy: God's love for the martyrs of the generation of repression, God's jealousy for Zion. Israel and God thus are embodied in the figures of Isaac, Esau, and Jacob, Jonathan, David, and Saul, and so on. The ultimate relationship is God and Israel, with Zion in the middle.

The formal program involves a phrase of Song of Songs, the subject of the sentence, and then an item drawn from the implicit virtues of attitude or action of the Rabbinic system. Here it is "I slept" plus predicate, "my heart was awake" plus predicate. Then the givens of the system emerge in the predicate of the entries to the list. The list-making program of Song of Songs Rabbah here joins together diverse virtues and imperatives in a single pattern:

SONG OF SONGS RABBAH LXII:I

1. A. "I slept, but my heart was awake (Song 5:2):"
   B. Said the Community of Israel before the Holy One, blessed be He, "Lord of the world, 'I slept:' as to the religious duties,
   C. "'but my heart was awake:' as to acts of loving kindness.
   D. "'I slept:' as to acts of righteousness.
   E. "'but my heart was awake:' in doing them.
   F. "'I slept:' as to the offerings.
   G. "'but my heart was awake:' as to reciting the *Shema* and saying the Prayer.
   H. "'I slept:' as to the house of the sanctuary.
   I. "'but my heart was awake:' as to synagogues and study-houses.
   J. "'I slept:' as to the end of days.
   K. "'but my heart was awake:' as to redemption.
   L. "'I slept:' as to redemption.
   M. "'but the heart' of the Holy One, blessed be He, 'was awake' to redeem me."

Here the repertoire of virtue is joined by a catalogue of contrasts: religious duties and acts of loving kindness, offerings and recitation of the *Shema* and the Prayer, house of the sanctuary and synagogues and study houses, end of days and redemption, The program of Rabbinic Judaism supplies the data for comparison and contrast. These simple selections supply the data we require to show how the Rabbinic program of norms is implicit throughout Song of Songs Rabbah.

The details should not obscure the larger picture: the presence of norms of behavior and belief that define Israel as distinct from the nations.

SONG OF SONGS RABBAH XIX:I

5. A. R. Azariah in the name of R. Judah in the name of R. Simon [interpreted the cited verse ['as a lily among brambles, so is my love among maidens' (Song 2:2)] to speak of Israel before Mount Sinai].

B. ["'a lily among brambles:'] The matter may be compared to a king who had an orchard. He planted in it rows upon rows of figs, grapevines, and pomegranates. After a while the king went down to his vineyard and found it filled with thorns and brambles. He brought woodcutters and cut it down. But he found in the orchard a single red rose. He took it and smelled it and regained his serenity and said, 'This rose is worthy that the entire orchard be saved on its account.'

C. "So too the entire world was created only on account of the Torah. For twenty-six generations the Holy One, blessed be He, looked down upon his world and saw it full of thorns and brambles, for example, the Generation of Enosh, the generation of the Flood, and the Sodomites.

D. "He planned to render the world useless and to destroy it: 'The Lord sat enthroned at the flood' (Ps. 29:10).

E. "But he found in the world a single red rose, Israel, that was destined to stand before Mount Sinai and to say before the Holy One, blessed be He, 'Whatever the Lord has said we shall do and we shall obey' (Ex. 24:7).

F. "Said the Holy One, blessed be He, [Lev. R.:] 'Israel is worthy that the entire world be saved on its account.'" [Song: "for the sake of the Torah and those who study it....."]

10. A. R. Abun said, "Just as a lily wilts so long as the hot spell persists, but when the dew falls on it, the lily thrives again,

B. "so Israel, so long as the shadow of Esau falls across the world, Israel wilts,

C. "but when the shadow of Esau passes from the world, Israel will once more thrive:

D. "'I shall be like the dew for Israel. It will blossom as the lily' (Hos. 14:6)."

11. A. Just as the lily expires only with its scent, so Israel expires only with religious acts and good deeds.

B. Just as the lily is only for the scent, so the righteous were created only for the redemption of Israel.

C. Just as the lily is placed on the table of kings at the beginning and end of a meal, so Israel will be in both this world and the world to come.

D. Just as it is easy to tell a lily from the thorns, so it is easy to tell the Israelites from the nations of the world.

E. That is in line with this verse of Scripture: "All those who see them will recognize them" (Isa. 61:9).

F. Just as a lily is made ready for Sabbaths and festivals, so Israel is made ready for the coming redemption.

G. R. Berekhiah said, "Said the Holy One, blessed be He, to Moses, 'Go and say to Israel My children, when you were in Egypt, you were like a lily among brambles. Now that you come into the land of Israel, you shall be like a lily among brambles.

Eight. Loving and Being Loved by, God: Song of Songs Rabbah

    H.   """Be careful not to do deeds like those of this party or that.'"
    I.   "Thus [Moses admonished Israel, saying to them, 'You shall not do as they do in the land of Egypt, where you dwelt, and you shall not do as they do in the land of Canaan, to which I am bringing you. You shall not walk in their statutes'" (Lev. 18:3).

The composition before us leaves no doubt that Israel in Rabbinic Judaism stands apart from the nations of the world and has nothing to do with them. XIX:i.5 has the world saved by Israel, the rose among the thorns. Israel's future loyalty to the Torah suffices. No. 10 has Israel wilt under Esau's shadow but revive when Esau passes. Then the Rabbinic way of life — religious acts and good deeds — figures. Israel is distinguished from the nations of the world. It prepares for the coming redemption by means of the Sabbath and festivals.

The implicit norms of inclusion and exclusion have registered their presence throughout. The sages who compiled Song of Songs Rabbah read the Song of Songs as a sequence of statements of urgent love between God and Israel, the holy people. How they convey in symbolic language the intensity of Israel's love of God forms the point of special interest in this document. For it is not in propositions that they choose to speak, but in the medium of symbols. That means the implicit norms emerge not as matters of theological assertion but issues of attitude and emotion. The sages set forth sequences of words that connote meanings, elicit emotions, stand for events, form the verbal equivalent of pictures or music or dance or poetry. Through the repertoire of these verbal-symbols and their arrangement and rearrangement, the message the authors wish to convey emerges: not in so many words, but through words nonetheless. Sages chose for their compilation a very brief list of items among many possible candidates. They therefore determined to appeal to a highly restricted list of implicit meanings, calling upon some very few events or persons, repeatedly identifying these as the expressions of God's profound affection for Israel, and Israel's deep love for God. The message of the document comes not so much from stories of what happened or did not happen, assertions of truth or denials of error, but rather from the repetitious rehearsal of sets of symbols.

The dogmas of Rabbinic Judaism, inclusive of those persons that conform to them, exclusive of those that do not, prove blatant. Song of Songs Rabbah through its lists provides the best evidence of the dogmatic definitions of Rabbinic Judaism in the entire formative canon. Its emphasis on the passionate connection between God and Israel embodied in the Torah, its commandments and convictions, attests to a well-constructed system. And its cogency testifies to the context of controversy in which the system was conceived. In the poetry of Song of Songs Rabbah we are able to reconstruct the character of the opposition of Rabbinic Judaism as the Rabbinic sages construed that opposition.

9

The Norms of Conviction of Rabbinic Judaism: Orthodoxy and Heresy

I. PRINCIPAL ELEMENTS OF ORTHODOX DOCTRINE

By "orthodox" here I mean, the normative theological system and its doctrines on particular issues put forth in the Rabbinic canon. By "heresy" I mean, positions contrary to those norms. We know who belongs to the community of correct doctrine, called by the canon "Israel," by identifying adherents to the implicit norms that animate the canonical writings of Rabbinic Judaism. We know who does not belong to that "Israel" by imagining the positions of those that contradict the norms.

But of whom do we speak? We do not know the state of public opinion among Jews of various kinds, nor can we assume that what the canon deems normative corresponds with actuality. We do know what the Rabbinic authorities set forth in their canon and can identify the fundamentals on which they formed their consensus. They acknowledge contrary opinion only rarely, and we have no documents produced outside of the Rabbinic circles that set forth contrary systems to the one laid out in the Rabbinic canon. So we deal with the Rabbinic account of matters and extrapolate from that the character of their (imagined) competition and opposition.

One thing is clear. The Rabbinic writings yield a cogent system, and implicitly they construct as a mirror-image an equally coherent contrary one. The Rabbinic system rests on the foundation that one God made heaven and earth and governs all things past, present and future. Belief in two or more gods is heresy. The narrative of Scripture and the laws and traditions set forth by the Rabbinic writings, one by one and all together, systematically explore the implications of the unity of God. Invoking documents that contradict Scripture and tradition signals heresy. Law and narrative present monotheism as a system of culture and a narrative as well: mythic monotheism realized in the Israelite social order. Denial of the systematic dominion of the one and only God marks the eretic. Rejection of the dogma of his justice and mercy, the dogma of God's responsibility for the Torah, of the dogma of resurrection for judgment at the end of days stigmatizes the heretic. So far as the Rabbinic writings speak of heresy, it is in the context of the orthodoxy framed by monotheism as sustained in the ancient Scriptures. Let us examine the principal parts of that system as these parts form the implicit outcomes of the documents we have selected.

ONE GOD. GOD'S UNITY EXPRESSED IN THE UNITY OF BEING: NATURE, SOCIETY, HISTORY, COSMOS: all things derive from one thing, and one thing yields all things. The Mishnah forms a concrete demonstration of the abstractions of monotheism. The scriptural account of the cosmos forms the generative categories, which constitute an ordered, hierarchical unity of being. Human events cohere as well, forming a testimony to the governance of history by the one God who made heaven and earth. A single set of principles governs through all time; Israel's history and also the history of the nations embody those principles, so Genesis Rabbah. Nature, history, and Israelite society join together to make a single statement in common, a statement of monotheism realized in the unity of the natural and the social and world order. Torah and the Temple, Torah-study and Temple-sacrifice — all conform to the same pattern, thus Leviticus Rabbah. God is not only benevolent but passionate; God weeps for Israel and shares in Israel's suffering. God mourns when Israel's deeds bring on disaster, Lamentations Rabbah maintains. Song of Songs Rabbah forms the climax of the monotheist exposition. God imposes the obligation to love, and be loved by, God: "You will love the Lord your God with all your heart, with all your soul, and with all your might."

THE TORAH: Sifra takes as premise the claim that the Torah contains God's words in God's own wording and so affords access to God's mind Torah-study in Abot forms the highest calling, because it brings disciples into direct contact with God, his word and his presence. Torah and Torah-learning form the matrix for all other expositions; a trait of the canon as a whole is the constant resort to proof-texts of Scripture.

ISRAEL: Israel is God's special love. That love is shown in a simple way. Israel's present condition of subordination derives from its own deeds. It follows that God cares, so Israel may look forward to redemption on God's part in response to Israel's own regeneration through repentance, so Leviticus Rabbah. So too, nature and supernature, earth and heaven, correlate and make a harmonious statement. The course of Israel on earth embodies the course of the moon and the solar seasons in heaven, and when Israel mends its way, all of astral nature will respond, thus Pesiqta deRab Kahana.

FREE WILL, RESPONSIBILITY, JUDGMENT, AND RESURRECTION: God is just and merciful. Tractate Abot takes for granted that God knows what all persons, endowed with free will and responsible for their exercise thereof, do and judges them, with eternal consequences for resurrection or for perpetual death.

RIGHT ATTITUDE AND EMOTIONS: An Israelite in the teaching of tractate Abot should accommodate his wishes to those of others. He should love God. What is required of Israel is submission to God and conciliation of one's fellow man. Other documents concur, but it is in tractate Abot that the matter is featured.

II. THE ORTHODOX DEFINITION OF HERESY

Monotheism in the Rabbinic context emerges in the initial documents as an abstraction.[1] The Mishnah and tractate Abot encompass in what is implicit the principles of monotheism. But they contain little of that dense mythic instantiation of God's rule in nature, history, society, and the celestial realm that would emerge in the later Midrash-compilations.

Abot defines heresy out of its affirmation of resurrection, judgment, and the Torah. These yield in the form of heresies: denial of the Torah, of judgment, and therefore of resurrection as critical to the Torah's construction of human existence. The Mishnah finds heresy in theories of the complexity of being, positing two powers in heaven for example, or distinguishing between and among sources of divine governance. Heretics will not concede the absolute One without distinction and without variety. Sifra will insist that the Torah comes from heaven and is the literal word of God, against the heresy that would attribute the Torah to human fabrication.

The conception that cogent rules do not govern human events but chaos brought on by conflicting actions of diverse gods prevails contradicts the premise of Genesis Rabbah that history reveals the one God's plan for all humanity. Nature follows its own rules, distinct from those that govern history and the social order; the social order does not present the occasion of sanctification, contrary to the position of Leviticus Rabbah and, for the separation of nature from history, Pesiqta deRab Kahana.

God does not respond to the love of the unique People, Israel, contrary to the view of Leviticus Rabbah. The stars in the heavens shape the destiny of humanity on earth, and Israel is governed by the stars just as much as are the gentiles, contrary to Pesiqta deRab Kahana. The God known in the Torah is malevolent and bears no good will for Israel, a Gnostic position that contradicts the point of insistence of Lamentations Rabbah. The malevolence of God for Israel is contradicted by the love of God for Israel instantiated in Song of Songs Rabbah.

All that is required for this characterization of heresy in the setting of Rabbinic Judaism accomplished in stating the opposite of the implicit norms of the canonical writings. A reading of the main points of the normative liturgy in the *Shema* and the Prayer yields a similar exposition of rejected propositions. That liturgy addresses the one God who hears and answers prayer. He creates the world, reveals the Torah, and redeems Israel. Denying the unity of being posited in the liturgy realizes the implicit heresy fabricated by the Rabbinic system. Whether within Israel or beyond its limits such a cogent heresy flourished is for others to determine. It suffices to say that the Rabbinic canon, start to finish, sets forth an exclusive claim to truth and dismisses as null all contrary claims.

III. BORDERLINES

From the very beginnings of the Rabbinic system in its preserved writings border lines distinguished Rabbinic Judaism from all other systemic responses to the same Scriptures that the ancient Rabbis invoked. This rapid survey yields an account of a religious system that from the outset defined both itself and its opposition. The canonical writings of Rabbinic Judaism attest to a fully articulated definition of theological norms and define an opposition-system as well.

Not only so, but those same main lines of those norms consistently surface in every document we have surveyed (as well as in the canonical documents we have not treated here, so I ask the reader to stipulate). Whether we turn to the Mishnah, ca. 200, or Abot, variously dated as early in the canonical process and as late, or Song of Songs Rabbah and Lamentations Rabbah, by consensus situated at an indeterminate point but probably toward the end of that same continuous process, the outcome is the same. Monotheism has imposed its logic, which has imparted cogency throughout. The symbolic structure of Rabbinic Judaism, with its mythic framing of monotheism, pervades, whether in the invocation of the Torah or in its account of God's participation in Israel's life. We discern at the foundations of every document a single cogent construction — the monotheist conception yielded by Scripture and systematized by the Rabbinic canon. Then each compilation in sequence takes up its particular burden within the composition of a complete and cogent statement.

And we have no problem imagining the opposed position, a negotiation that yields less than the monotheist logic of the Rabbinic system: the rejectionist and heretical one. That is so even though we can hardly match the Rabbinic system founded in the bedrock of mythic monotheism with a single contrary system, whether Christian or pagan, resting on other foundations altogether, e.g., two powers in heaven against the datum of Pesiqta deRab Kahana. The upshot is, from its earliest documentary evidence to the latest of late antiquity, a single system of myth and symbol, law and theology, defined Rabbinic Judaism and distinguished that Judaism from all other religious systems, originating in communities of Judaic, Christian, or pagan venues, whether resting on Scripture or rejecting Scripture altogether. We need hardly ask for the testimony, as to the norms, of articulate sayings, e.g., concerning the unity of God, the justice and mercy of God, the origin with God of the Torah and the origin in the Torah of the critical doctrine of resurrection, judgment, and the restoration of Eden and life eternal. The entire set of statements of successive composites attests to those same definitive norms of conviction.

Accordingly, Rabbinic Judaism defined itself and designated its opposition. It accomplished the partition of its system from all other, competing ones, whether

Nine. The Norms of Conviction of Rabbinic Judaism: Orthodoxy and Heresy

near at hand or remote, and this it did from its earliest writings to the latest ones of late antiquity. What shifted from the Mishnah to the concluding Midrash-compilations is not the theological norm, the paramount dogma, but only its expression in ever more human terms.

This emergent view of a fully-exposed Judaic religious system, distinct from the very start to the indeterminate finish from all other Judaisms and Christianities and paganisms of late antiquity, bears implications not to be missed. It portrays Rabbinic Judaism as completely realized but for secondary articulation in the Mishnah and present in all subsequent writings. And it yields the presence of both orthodoxy and heresy in the context of formative Rabbinic Judaism from its earliest writings to its climactic statement in the Bavli, the Talmud of Babylonia. That Judaic system emerges in these pages as an inclusionary and exclusionary construction of implicit norms constituting the bedrock of what became normative Judaism. The system says as much in so many words at its critical moment, the declaration of eternal life as the fate of all Israel with a few important exceptions — e.g., those that deny the Torah is from heaven. But we have seen that the system forms the bed rock of the classical writings of that same Judaism. The ancient Rabbis knew who belonged and who did not belong to the Israel that would rise from the grave for eternal life. It goes without saying that Rabbinic Judaism by the canonical writings surveyed here drew border lines between the Torah, which we call in more secular language "Judaism" and the communities of Christianity with whom it shared some sacred Scriptures.

Daniel Boyarin has set forth a different view of the same matter of the separation, from Christianity, of the Torah as Rabbinic Judaism portrayed it.[2] A brief account of his thesis will clarify the issues. Boyarin's account of Judaism defines the frame of reference here, even though he deals with Christianity as well: "Even Rabbinic Judaism was struggling to figure out for itself what a 'Judaism' is and who then could be defined as in and out of it" (p. xi). "Authorities on both sides [Judaism, Christianity] tried to establish a border, a line that, when crossed, meant that someone had definitively left one group for another" (p. 2). That line, we have observed, crossed the grave. The Israelite who crossed the line joined the permanently dead.

Boyarin continues, "...Rabbinic texts project a nascent and budding heresiology..." (p. 5). Boyarin stresses the theme of the *minim* (p. 5) and lays emphasis upon the difference between Judaism and Christianity: "the difference between Christianity and Judaism is not so much a difference between two religions as a difference between a religion and an entity that refuses to be one" (p. 8). Quite what is meant here is difficult to say, since Christian orthodox doctrine and Rabbinic orthodox doctrine focus on an agendum of issues common to them both and deriving from the same Scripture; if Christianity conforms to a programmatic model, Judaism responds to the same set of questions. But in the end Boyarin leaves no doubt as to his meaning:

The argument of this book is that ... at the first stage of its existence, at the time of the initial formulation of Rabbinic Judaism, the Rabbis...did seriously attempt to construct Judaism...as an orthodoxy and thus as a 'religion,' the product of disembedding of certain realms of practice, speech, and so on from others and identifying them as of particular circumstance. If you do not believe such and such or practice so and so, you are not a Jew, imply the texts of the period. At a later stage, however,...at the stage of the 'definitive' formulation of Rabbinic Judaism in the Babylonian Talmud, the Rabbis rejected this option, proposing instead the distinct ecclesiological principle that 'an Israelite, even if he...sins, remains an Israelite.' The historical layering of these two ideologies and even self-definitions by the Rabbis themselves of what it is that constitutes an Israel and an Israelite provide for the creative ambivalence in the status of Judaism today...." (p. 10).

This notion of "religion" as disembedded would await the Protestant Reformation for full articulation. But that is not our problem. Boyarin wishes to differentiate the Bavli's system from that of the prior canonical documents. I see several problems in his thesis.

First, the documents we have examined contain no judgment upon the status of Israelites who reject principles of practice or belief, except the Mishnah's statement, to which we have referred many times, that all Israel has a portion in the world to come except.... That statement comes *at the very outset* of the Rabbinic canon, in the earliest of its documents beyond Scripture. Then "Israel" is constituted by those destined to enjoy life eternal. Even those that sin are included (with the stated exceptions in mind). There were other theologies produced by other Judaic systems; the library at Qumran presents an exclusivist theory of who is Israel and who is not.

But, second, that is not because of a paramount latitudinarianism uncharacteristic of the earlier documents and surfacing only at the end to be adopted by the Talmud of Babylonia. All Israel has a portion in the world to come because death atones for sin, and Israelites die sinless. Hence at issue at Mishnah-tractate Sanhedrin 11:1 is only the exceptions to the prevailing norm that death atones for sin and leaves the Israelite sinless in judgment. That is why by the definition of Israel of Rabbinic Judaism — those that live eternally — the sinful Israelite remains an Israelite, that is, will stand in judgment.

That definition of who and what is Israel accounts for the latitudinarian judgment of Rabbinic Judaism — and its power. The matter is explicit at M. Sanhedrin 6:2:

Mishnah-tractate Sanhedrin 6:2

A. [When] he was ten cubits from the place of stoning, they say to him, "Confess," for it is usual for those about to be put to death to confess.

B. For whoever confesses has a share in the world to come.

C. For so we find concerning Achan, to whom Joshua said, "My son, I pray you, give glory to the Lord, the God of Israel, and confess to him, [and tell me now what you have done; hide it not from me.] And Achan answered Joshua and said, Truly have I sinned against the Lord, the God of Israel, and thus and thus I have done" (Josh. 7:19). And how do we know that his confession achieved atonement for him? For it is said, "And Joshua said, Why have you troubled us? The Lord will trouble you this day" (Josh. 7:25) — This day you will be troubled, but you will not be troubled in the world to come.

D. And if he does not know how to confess, they say to him, "Say as follows: 'Let my death be atonement for all of my transgressions.'"

The clear implication of this teaching of the Mishnah is that Achan's death atones for his sin, and consequently he enters the world to come with nearly all Israelites. The Bavli understands the passage in exactly the way I have interpreted the Mishnah's statement:

II.1 A. And how do we know that his confession achieved atonement for him [M. 6:2C]?
B. *Our rabbis have taught on Tannaite authority:*
C. And how do we know that his confession achieved atonement for him?
D. For it is said, "And Joshua said, Why have you troubled us? The Lord will trouble you this day"] (Josh. 7:25).

III.1 A. "This day you are troubled, but you will not be troubled in the world to come" [M. 6:2C].
B. And it is written, "And the sons of Zerah are Zimri, Ethan, Heman, Calcol, Darda, five in all" (1 Chr. 2:6).
C. What is the sense of "five in all"?
D. They are five in all destined for the world to come [cf. T. San. 9:5D-F].
E. Here it is Zimri, but elsewhere Achan [Josh. 7:24].
F. Rab and Samuel:
G. One said, "His name was Achan, and why was he called Zimri? Because he acted like Zimri."
H. The other said, 'His name was Zimri, and why was he called Achan? Because he [Schachter:] wound the sins of Israel about them like a serpent [Achan = snake in Greek, echidna]."

Ethnicity, indelible or otherwise, in light of this discussion is not what is at stake in the Rabbinic formulation of the Bavli, "an Israelite, even though he sins, remains an Israelite," and the definition of "Judaism" as a "religion" is not at issue. Indeed, how the Rabbinic sages would have received so anachronistic a social category as "ethnicity" as distinct from a "religion" and in what context they would have contemplated such a template for their doctrine of "Israel" form matters that do not emerge in Boyarin's narrative.

The reason that Israelites even though they have sinned remain Israelites encompasses the definition of Israelites that pertains: they are those who inherit the world to come and have a portion in the restored Eden. Their sins are atoned for by their death, and the world to come awaits. Death marks the final atonement for sin, which bears its implication for the condition of man at the resurrection. Because one has atoned through sin (accompanied at the hour of death by a statement of repentance, "May my death be atonement for all my sins," in the liturgy in due course), when he is raised from the dead, his atonement for all his sins is complete. He cannot cease to be an Israelite, to belong to Israel. The judgment after resurrection becomes for most a formality. That is why "all Israel has a portion in the world to come," with the exception of a few whose sins are not atoned for by death, and that is by their own word. That is the position of Rabbinic Judaism from the Mishnah forward, and the Talmud of Babylonia does not innovate and mark a new and different theology (Boyarin's ideology) at all. We cannot speak as Boyarin does of a "historical layering "...of what constitutes an Israel and an Israelite...." (p. 10). The sequence of documents sustains an account not of layering but of logical succession, refinement and articulation of givens announced in the earlier documents and amplified n the later ones.

Boyarin is explicit in his view that "in the end — at least in the end of late antiquity — Rabbinic Judaism refused the option of becoming a religion, another species of the kind that Christianity offered. At the final stage of the development of classical Rabbinism, a reassertion of the 'locative' of identity as given and not as achieved — or lost — came to be emblematic of Judaism" (p. 12). So Boyarin concludes, "Judaism is not and has not been, since early in the Christian era, a 'religion' in the sense of an orthodoxy whereby heterodox views...would make one an outsider..." (p. 13). Judaism, Boyarin says, rejected "the option of orthodoxy and heresy as the Jews' mode of self-definition...the refusal...finally to become and be a religion" (p. 13). For late antiquity, Boyarin imposes categories of his own and ignores the implicit affirmations of the Rabbinic sources. To what "Jews" he refers when he speaks of modes of "self-definition," I cannot say. I can only repeat that for the "Israel" represented by the Rabbinic canonical documents, from the Mishnah through the Bavli, "Judaism" meaning the religious system of the social order set forth by those documents qualifies as a religion that excludes and that includes by the criteria of orthodoxy and heresy, like any other religion.

The Rabbinic documents surveyed here — the Mishnah and the Tosefta — accordingly fall into Boyarin's classification of the age of orthodoxy, and they certainly do presuppose theological premises we may categorize as exclusive and normative. But the differentiation of the Bavli's definitions — rejecting the notion of orthodoxy altogether, as Boyarin claims, in favor of indelible ethnicity — from those of the earlier orthodox documents proves dubious. Boyarin misconstrues the character of the Bavli viewed whole. His arguments from isolated texts carry no probative weight.

The Bavli extends the Mishnah's and Tosefta's and the other received sets of laws and principles. It articulates and instantiates and harmonizes those laws and principles, it does not subvert them. More to the point, those early documents make provision for sinful Israelites, who remain Israel in the exact sense: those that will rise from the grave. There is no open space between the Mishnah's and Tosefta's definition of the status of the sinful Israelite and that prevailing in Lamentations Rabbah, Song of Songs Rabbah, and as a matter of fact also in the two Talmuds, not surveyed in these pages. No other definition of "Israel" surfaces in these later documents, and the shibboleth about the sinful Israelite remaining an Israelite does not for one minute contradict that statement of the Mishnah's and the Tosefta's but confirms it. Rabbinic Judaism sets forth a religious system that, systemically, is not to be distinguished in its basic model and pattern from Christianity: both are religions within the same model and pattern of what is meant by religion. Debates on who constitutes the true Israel do not change the picture. Every account in late antique Judaic writings of what Israel is and who qualifies for membership or is excluded from belonging presupposes that to belong to Israel treats belonging to Israel as a supernatural affiliation, and Israel as a religious category-formation of the social order.[3]

Furthermore, the distinction between religion and ethnicity conflicts with the profoundly religious character of the Bavli's system. By religious character I mean, the character of a system that situates God at the heart of matters and invokes God's presence throughout. A religion asks the social order to realize the will of God. A religion identifies as critical matters the truth-claims of the faithful. Rabbinic Judaism as sealed by the Bavli qualifies as a religion, not a secular ethnicity, on all counts.

The law that the Bavli amplifies and harmonizes, the narratives that it sets forth, the prophecy and exhortation that its principals engage in — the Bavli as a whole is permeated by the vivid faith in God's presence and passionate concern for all Israelites individually, and for corporate Israel as a unique moral entity in humanity. The Bavli, no less than the Mishnah or Song of Songs Rabbah or Lamentations Rabbah, contemplates a world in which God is everywhere present. Simply comparing the Bavli's treatment of Mishnah- and Tosefta-tractate Berakhot suffices to call into question Boyarin's distinction between the Bavli and the Mishnah and the other documents from the Mishnah to the Bavli.

I challenge Boyarin to point to a single composition in the Bavli in which an ethnic group, the Jews or the Jewish people, its this-worldly preservation and its cultural continuity, defined what was at stake without regard to God's purpose and God's will for all humanity. In the eight documents considered here we found variations on a single theme, and the Bavli yields ample instances of reworking the same theme: God's love for Israel and Israel's vocation to respond to that love.

Boyarin commits gross anachronism. Ethnicity and "Jewishness" in place of religiosity and Judaism would make their entry only much later, first in the figure of Spinoza, then in the quest for an ethnic foundation for a nation state in Zionism, and finally in the formation, in the aftermath of the Holocaust, of an utterly ethnic consciousness sustained by a secular myth of Holocaust and Redemption in late twentieth century American Jewry. Invoking those categories for the Rabbinic Judaic system of late antiquity represents an act of anachronism. Specifically, the categories of ethnicity and nationality come into play many, many centuries later, in the nineteenth and twentieth centuries to be exact, when the Jew who denies Judaism yet remains a Jew by ethnic identification — the "unJewish Jew" of Isaac Deutscher for example — makes an appearance. Then, but not in the pages of the Bavli, "Israel" came to stand locatively for the state of Israel rather than for the utopian people of God.

The generative questions answered by norms of belief, inclusive of criteria for exclusion, find the same answers in every canonical document from the Mishnah through the Bavli. They are as follows: What right doctrines form the foundation of the theology of the human condition — what it means to be a human being — in Abot? What are the dogmas that govern the demonstration and organization of knowledge in the Mishnah? How to sort out the interplay of reason and revelation in Sifra? What are the lessons of history and how is Israel to make sense of contemporary events in Genesis Rabbah? What imperatives govern the sanctification of Israel beyond time in Leviticus Rabbah? How does the Israelite experience God and what does he know about God in Song of Songs Rabbah and Lamentations Rabbah, respectively? The answers to these questions early and late in the formative canon define the premises of thought characteristic of Rabbinic Judaism, its orthodox norms, its concomitant designation of heresy too. Any claim that the Bavli parted company from the entire prior canonical repertoire will have to show how the Bavli stood against the entire received heritage of normative law and normative theology. I maintain that such a demonstration contradicts the character of the documents. Merely citing a sentence out of all context that affirms the Israel-ness of all Israelites, inclusive of sinners, scarcely suffices. The Bavli's documentary position begins in the whole, not in episodic bits and pieces of this and that. In context that statement of which so much is made by Boyarin conforms to the received system viewed whole: atoning through death for sins committed in life Israelites die sinless and inherit the world to come that awaits nearly all Israel in the end of days. That defines what is at stake in the Rabbinic system, that affirmation of eternal life inhering in all Israel and in corporate Israel as well.[4]

ENDNOTES

[1] In Chapter One I have already called attention to the problem of dating Abot. The present discussion includes Abot in accord with the present consensus.
[2] Daniel Boyarin, *Border Lines. The Partition of Judaeo-Christianity* (Philadelphia, 2004: University of Pennsylvania Press).
[3] *Judaism and its Social Metaphors. Israel in the History of Jewish Thought.* N.Y., 1988: Cambridge University Press.
[4] I refer to *The Social Teaching of Rabbinic Judaism.* 2001: E. J. Brill. I. *Corporate Israel and the Individual Israelite.* II. *Between Israelites.* III. *God's Presence in Israel.*

STUDIES IN JUDAISM
TITLES IN THE SERIES
PUBLISHED BY UNIVERSITY PRESS OF AMERICA

Judith Z. Abrams
The Babylonian Talmud: A Topical Guide, 2002.

Roger David Aus
Matthew 1-2 and the Virginal Conception: In Light of Palestinian and Hellenistic Judaic Traditions on the Birth of Israel's First Redeemer, Moses, 2004.

My Name Is "Legion": Palestinian Judaic Traditions in Mark 5:1-20 and Other Gospel Texts, 2003.

Alan L. Berger, Harry James Cargas, and Susan E. Nowak
The Continuing Agony: From the Carmelite Convent to the Crosses at Auschwitz, 2004.

S. Daniel Breslauer
Creating a Judaism without Religion: A Postmodern Jewish Possibility, 2001.

Bruce Chilton
Targumic Approaches to the Gospels: Essays in the Mutual Definition of Judaism and Christianity, 1986.

David Ellenson
Tradition in Transition: Orthodoxy, Halakhah, and the Boundaries of Modern Jewish Identity, 1989.

Paul V. M. Flesher
New Perspectives on Ancient Judaism, Volume 5: Society and Literature in Analysis, 1990.

Marvin Fox
Collected Essays on Philosophy and on Judaism, Volume One: Greek Philosophy, Maimonides, 2003.

Collected Essays on Philosophy and on Judaism, Volume Two: Some Philosophers, 2003.

Collected Essays on Philosophy and on Judaism, Volume Three: Ethics, Reflections, 2003.

Zev Garber
Methodology in the Academic Teaching of Judaism, 1986.

Zev Garber, Alan L. Berger, and Richard Libowitz
Methodology in the Academic Teaching of the Holocaust, 1988.

Abraham Gross
Spirituality and Law: Courting Martyrdom in Christianity and Judaism, 2005.

Harold S. Himmelfarb and Sergio DellaPergola
Jewish Education Worldwide: Cross-Cultural Perspectives, 1989.

William Kluback
The Idea of Humanity: Hermann Cohen's Legacy to Philosophy and Theology, 1987.

Samuel Morell
Studies in the Judicial Methodology of Rabbi David ibn Abi Zimra, 2004.

Jacob Neusner
Ancient Israel, Judaism, and Christianity in Contemporary Perspective, 2006.

The Aggadic Role in Halakhic Discourses: Volume I, 2001.

The Aggadic Role in Halakhic Discourses: Volume II, 2001.

The Aggadic Role in Halakhic Discourses: Volume III, 2001.

Analysis and Argumentation in Rabbinic Judaism, 2003.

Analytical Templates of the Bavli, 2006.

Ancient Judaism and Modern Category-Formation: "Judaism," "Midrash," "Messianism," and Canon in the Past Quarter Century, 1986.

Canon and Connection: Intertextuality in Judaism, 1987.

Chapters in the Formative History of Judaism. 2006

Dual Discourse, Single Judaism, 2001.

The Emergence of Judaism: Jewish Religion in Response to the Critical Issues of the First Six Centuries, 2000.

First Principles of Systemic Analysis: The Case of Judaism within the History of Religion, 1988.

The Halakhah and the Aggadah, 2001.

Halakhic Hermeneutics, 2003.

Halakhic Theology: A Sourcebook, 2006.

The Hermeneutics of Rabbinic Category Formations, 2001.

How Important Was the Destruction of the Second Temple in the Formation of Rabbinic Judaism? 2006.

How Not to Study Judaism, Examples and Counter-Examples, Volume One: Parables, Rabbinic Narratives, Rabbis' Biographies, Rabbis' Disputes, 2004.

How Not to Study Judaism, Examples and Counter-Examples, Volume Two: Ethnicity and Identity versus Culture and Religion, How Not to Write a Book on Judaism, Point and Counterpoint, 2004.

How the Halakhah Unfolds: Moed Qatan in the Mishnah, ToseftaYerushalmi and Bavli, 2006.

The Implicit Norms of Rabbinic Judaism. 2006.

Intellectual Templates of the Law of Judaism, 2006.

Is Scripture the Origin of the Halakhah? 2005.

Israel and Iran in Talmudic Times: A Political History, 1986.

Israel's Politics in Sasanian Iran: Self-Government in Talmudic Times, 1986.

Judaism in Monologue and Dialogue, 2005.

Major Trends in Formative Judaism, Fourth Series, 2002.

Major Trends in Formative Judaism, Fifth Series, 2002.

Messiah in Context: Israel's History and Destiny in Formative Judaism, 1988.

The Native Category - Formations of the Aggadah: The Later Midrash-Compilations - Volume I, 2000.

The Native Category - Formations of the Aggadah: The Earlier Midrash-Compilations - Volume II, 2000.

Paradigms in Passage: Patterns of Change in the Contemporary Study of Judaism, 1988.

Parsing the Torah, 2005.

Praxis and Parable: The Divergent Discourses of Rabbinic Judaism, 2006.

The Religious Study of Judaism: Description, Analysis and Interpretation, Volume 1, 1986.

The Religious Study of Judaism: Description, Analysis, Interpretation, Volume 2, 1986.

The Religious Study of Judaism: Context, Text, Circumstance, Volume 3, 1987.

The Religious Study of Judaism: Description, Analysis, Interpretation, Volume 4: Ideas of History, Ethics, Ontology, and Religion in Formative Judaism, 1988.

Struggle for the Jewish Mind: Debates and Disputes on Judaism Then and Now, 1988.

The Talmud Law, Theology, Narrative: A Sourcebook, 2005.

Talmud Torah: Ways to God's Presence through Learning: An Exercise in Practical Theology, 2002.

Texts Without Boundaries: Protocols of Non-Documentary Writing in the Rabbinic Canon: Volume I: The Mishnah, Tractate Abot, and the Tosefta, 2002.

Texts Without Boundaries: Protocols of Non-Documentary Writing in the Rabbinic Canon: Volume II: Sifra and Sifré to Numbers, 2002.

Texts Without Boundaries: Protocols of Non-Documentary Writing in the Rabbinic Canon: Volume III: Sifré to Deuteronomy and Mekhilta Attributed to Rabbi Ishmael, 2002.

Texts Without Boundaries: Protocols of Non-Documentary Writing in the Rabbinic Canon: Volume IV: Leviticus Rabbah, 2002.

A Theological Commentary to the Midrash - Volume I: Pesiqta deRab Kahana, 2001.

A Theological Commentary to the Midrash - Volume II: Genesis Raba, 2001.

A Theological Commentary to the Midrash - Volume III: Song of Songs Rabbah, 2001.

A Theological Commentary to the Midrash - Volume IV: Leviticus Rabbah, 2001.

A Theological Commentary to the Midrash - Volume V: Lamentations Rabbati, 2001.

A Theological Commentary to the Midrash - Volume VI: Ruth Rabbah and Esther Rabbah, 2001.

A Theological Commentary to the Midrash - Volume VII: Sifra, 2001.

A Theological Commentary to the Midrash - Volume VIII: Sifré to Numbers and Sifré to Deuteronomy, 2001.

A Theological Commentary to the Midrash - Volume IX: Mekhilta Attributed to Rabbi Ishmael, 2001.

Theological Dictionary of Rabbinic Judaism: Part One: Principal Theological Categories, 2005.

Theological Dictionary of Rabbinic Judaism: Part Two: Making Connections and Building Constructions, 2005.

Theological Dictionary of Rabbinic Judaism: Part Three: Models of Analysis, Explanation, and Anticipation, 2005.

Theology of Normative Judaism: A Source Book, 2005.

The Torah and the Halakhah: The Four Relationships, 2003.

The Unity of Rabbinic Discourse: Volume I: Aggadah in the Halakhah, 2001.

The Unity of Rabbinic Discourse: Volume II: Halakhah in the Aggadah, 2001.

The Unity of Rabbinic Discourse: Volume III: Halakhah and Aggadah in Concert, 2001.

*The Vitality of Rabbinic Imagination: The Mishnah Against the Bible and Qumran,*2005.

Who, Where and What is "Israel?": Zionist Perspectives on Israeli and American Judaism, 1989.
The Wonder-Working Lawyers of Talmudic Babylonia: The Theory and Practice of Judaism in its Formative Age, 1987.

Jacob Neusner and Ernest S. Frerichs
New Perspectives on Ancient Judaism, Volume 2: Judaic and Christian Interpretation of Texts: Contents and Contexts, 1987.

New Perspectives on Ancient Judaism, Volume 3: Judaic and Christian Interpretation of Texts: Contents and Contexts, 1987.

Jacob Neusner and James F. Strange
Religious Texts and Material Contexts, 2001.

David Novak and Norbert M. Samuelson
Creation and the End of Days: Judaism and Scientific Cosmology, 1986.

Proceedings of the Academy for Jewish Philosophy, 1990.

Aaron D. Panken
The Rhetoric of Innovation: Self-Conscious Legal Change in Rabbinic Literature, 2005.

Norbert M. Samuelson
Studies in Jewish Philosophy: Collected Essays of the Academy for Jewish Philosophy, 1980-1985, 1987.

Benjamin Edidin Scolnic
Alcimus, Enemy of the Maccabees, 2004.

If the Egyptians Drowned in the Red Sea Where are Pharaoh's Chariots?: Exploring the Historical Dimension of the Bible, 2005.

Rivka Ulmer
Pesiqta Rabbati: A Synoptic Edition of Pesiqta Rabbati Based upon all Extant Manuscripts and the Editio Princeps, Volume III, 2002.

Manfred H. Vogel
A Quest for a Theology of Judaism: The Divine, the Human and the Ethical Dimensions in the Structure-of-Faith of Judaism Essays in Constructive, 1987.

Anita Weiner
Renewal: Reconnecting Soviet Jewry to the Soviet People: A Decade of American Jewish Joint Distribution Committee (AJJDC) Activities in the Former Soviet Union 1988-1998, 2003.

Eugene Weiner and Anita Weiner
Israel-A Precarious Sanctuary: War, Death and the Jewish People, 1989.

The Martyr's Conviction: A Sociological Analysis, 2002.

Leslie S. Wilson
The Serpent Symbol in the Ancient Near East: Nahash and Asherah: Death, Life, and Healing, 2001.

www.ingramcontent.com/pod-product-compliance
Lightning Source LLC
Chambersburg PA
CBHW030116010526
44116CB00005B/271